Recolle
Poems For Every Occasion

Marcia JD Blair

ISBN: 978-976-96398-7-4

Book cover design by Christopher Lawrence - Logomeplease.

Printed by Kindle Direct Publishing, in the United States of America.

First printing edition 2021.

Anointed Writers Publishing
theanointedwriterjm@gmail.com
876-882-2691

www.theanointedwriter.com

I express sincere gratitude to all the persons who contributed to this project.

Thanks to the Most-High God, who made it possible, through the talents and. abilities he has so freely given. He has guided this work of art from its conception to the end.

A warm thank you is also extended to the leaders and members of Christian Fellowship World Outreach and Eastwood Park New Testament Church of God for their kind support.

Thanks to the nurses at the National Chest Hospital and The Victoria Jubilee Hospital, especially Nurse Bruce, Nurse Wallace and Nurse Harvey-Whittaker, Sister M. Miller, Sister Baines-Harley, Nurse Barrett-Young, Nurse Prehay, Nurse Tudor, Nurse J. Clarke and Nurse M. Francis; for their enthusiasm and kind encouragement.

A warm thank you to the Anointed Writers Publishing House for quality assurance and for such a remarkable and qualitative publication.

Finally, special thanks to my dear husband and friend, Garfield A. Blair, my daughter Tameica Blair, my son Jordan Blair, and my cousin Nikita Ducran who assisted with typing. They have all been exceptionally supportive and understanding!

Thanks again, to you all. You have helped to make this project not only a reality but a resounding success!

TABLE OF CONTENTS

Chapter 1

Appreciation & Retirement

Most Excellent is Your Name!

It is indeed a blessed honour
To face your golden years
As we try to wish you farewell
Our thoughts are mixed with tears!

With dignity, you laboured
You served with your whole heart
Because you were not selfish
So many values you impart!

Your work speaks loudly for you
You have made your mark
Touching the lives of others
You add a special spark!

You have been a faithful servant
Not seeking praise or fame
We love you and we thank you
"Most Excellent" is your name!

A Faithful Worker!

You have been a faithful worker
We could always count on you
Your loyal years of service
Tells you were keen and true!

You have been a faithful steward
Your reward comes not from man
The quality service that you gave
Showed others that they can...!

You have been a faithful employee
You light up your working world
You extended yourself to others
You must be a special kind of pearl!

You have been a faithful Civil Servant
You served with your whole heart
With dedication and interest
You have done your part!

A Faithful Servant!

You have been a faithful Servant,
You use each talent well,
For you regard your master,
His vineyard you won't sell!

You have been a faithful Servant,
Your reward no man can steal,
Your dedication and commitment
Shows the passion that you feel!

You have been a faithful Servant,
Pouring out your heart of love
Following God's clear direction,
You are an angel from above!

You have been a faithful Servant
Without complain, you do your part
Touching all the lives you can
With a sweet and tender heart!

Your Helping Hand!

You always lend a helping hand
And often help us understand
That God is always by our side
With arms of love that's opened wide!

We looked toward your helping hand
And saw the ground on which you stand
Sprinkled there was love unfeigned
It showed the grace of God you gained!

God has blessed your helping hand
That helps us through this pilgrim's land
You are a mother in our hearts
In our lives, you play great parts!

Thank you for your helping hand
You are shining in God's band
We never have to walk alone
Because of the kindness you have shown!

You Have Been Inspiring!

You have been humbled, innovative and sensational
And I'm so proud of you
You have blessed me with your kindness
This is found in just a few!

You have been creative, dynamic and encouraging
And I'm so impressed by you
You have touched the lives of many
The Lord confirms this too!

You have been a humming bird, with your inspiration
And I'm thanking God for you
You taught me to sing, relax and enjoy music
When I was sad, or down and blue!

You have been a talented and dedicated singer
And I'm so thrilled by you
You melt my heart within me
Your long years of service tells us you are true!

My Gracious Supervisor!

Hello, my warm and Gracious Supervisor
I just have to let you know
That the warmness of your persona
Daily makes me glow!

Hi, my Wonderful Guide and Leader
You are a source of strength to me
Your caring nature and your laughter
Filters all the beauty that I see!

Greetings, my Sweet and Special Superior
I appreciate your kind and loving ways
The way you relate to me and others
Really helps me through these days!

Blessings, my Loyal and Royal Director
You are firm, yet thoughtful and nice
Wrapped up inside your heart
Is a Gift of Sugar and Spice!

You Are So Outstanding

You are so outstanding, this we surely know
Evidenced by the hard work and commitment that you show
With determination, you have come this far
"Par Excellence" describes exactly how you!

To bestow on you great honour, is why we're here today
You deserve more glorious praises, than we can ever say
Over the years, with distinction, you have served
And your strength God has preserved!

God is your rewarder, never be dismayed
You are appreciated, for us you often prayed
We will always remember, the values you have taught
Our lives are surely moulded by the qualities you brought!

You cannot be forgotten; you served with your whole heart
Deep within our hearts, we know you did your part
As staff members, we salute you; you're always doing your best
God keeps you so empowered and victorious at each test!

A Devoted Christian

We bestow on you great honour
You have served throughout the years
And as we sadly watch you leave us
We have thoughts of joys and tears!

As choristers we salute you
For you have a gracious heart
You have blessed us with your singing
With joy you did your part!

Being so devoted; you're such a part of us
You have been a blessing; you sacrificed so much
With broken hearts, we miss you
You have such a loving touch!

You are always in God's service
You have engraved your mark
Touching the lives of others
You took some from the dark!

Doctor, You Are Honoured!

Thank you for helping me with so much sincerity
Indeed, you are honoured, I wish you prosperity
Words are so limited, to express how I feel
Your dedicated service is genuine and real!

Compassion and grace, characterize your persona
Perseverance and interest are always your aroma
You always care about my general health
May God bless you and give you great wealth!

I am much improved because of God and you
Your kind of commitment is found in just a few
I'll give you the roses while you are alive
To show appreciation is the way I thrive!

You have been there; through my pain and tears
To help me overcome my illness and fears
You are a doctor who made a difference
By your faithfulness and purest conscience!

On Your Retirement

On your retirement, we wish you all God's blessings
No more work; you're done with all the stressing
Throughout the years; your mind will stay refreshing
As love and kindness your heart always expressing!

On your retirement, you look so very young
As Godliness, you breathe in through your lung
Angels applaud you and heavenly songs they sung
Together, we cheer you on and there in love you clung!

On your retirement, please accept this token from us all
The memories that you leave with us are standing out so tall
The kind of service you have rendered, will keep us on the ball
And we dare to tell you, it is on our Facebook wall!

On your retirement, we miss you, some even cried
Your work was so distinctive, this you could not hide
You've impacted lives with greatest joy and pride
Touching lives with arms that's opened wide!

I Am Not

I am not retiring
I am just refiring
Neither am I resigning
I am just refiring!

I am not departing
I am only starting
Neither am I disheartening
I am really smartening!

I am not spilling
I am just refilling
Neither am I leaking
I am surely peaking!

I am not debating
Not even commentating
I am just meditating
God's word is saturating!

I am not degenerating
I am just regenerating
Not dead; not refrigerating
I am here, just reiterating!

I am not leaving
I am only cleaving
Neither am I bereaving
I am happily breathing!

I am not ending
I am just ascending
Neither am I depending
I am just transcending!

I am not declining
I am just rewinding
Neither am I descending
I am just re-blending!

I am not collapsing
I am just relaxing
Neither am I relapsing
And all my money retaxing!

I am not dying
Not even crying
Nor in bed lying
On my feet I'm trying!

A Kind and Caring Doctor!

You have been a kind and caring doctor
And l am so proud of you
I'm thrilled by your dedication
This is found in just a few!

You have been a faithful and thoughtful doctor
Not just thinking of yourself
You have served with all your kindness
I have proven this myself!

You have been a special and precious doctor
Having gone beyond the call of duty
You helped during my daughter's death and illness
Showing your deepest care and beauty!

You have been a humbled and gracious doctor
Always aiming to do your best
All your patients proudly thank you
from the north, south, east and west!

A Faithful Leader & Member!

You have been a long-standing member
Serving from January through to December
Your smile we will always remember
You have made your mark as a Star Member!

You have been with us from foundation
Hard working is your recommendation
This church is your accommodation
Enjoy the oneness or consolidation!

You have been loyal in your service
With you, we feel such loving bliss
With your wisdom, we cannot go amiss
God called you for such a time as this!

Thank you for being a fine leader
And for being such a great believer
Since Christ is your redeemer
You deserve a space in the Sunday Gleaner!

A Dedicated Missionary!

You have been a dedicated Missionary
And I thank God for you
You are truly a great example
Your love is always fresh and new!

You have been a full time Christian
Living up to the mark of God
You have blessed the lives of many
As you stretch out your scriptural rod!

You have been a devoted member
Through thick and thin you thrive
The interest you have in God's work
Shows Jesus is alive!

You have been a faithful servant
Not seeking praise from men
We all cherish you and honour you
The whole Church shout, "Amen"!

You are so Outstanding!

You are so outstanding
This is clear for all to see
You serve God with excitement
And often worship on your knee!

You are so outstanding
You are ahead of all the rest
Your faithful years of service
Shows you are highly blest!

You are so outstanding
We can always depend on you
You are a qualitative kind of person
So profound, so kind and true!

You are so outstanding
You are a blessing in this church
You are like a fruitful tree
On which all birds can perch!

You're Loyal and Faithful!

Dignity and gracefulness
Characterize your persona
Humility and thoughtfulness
Is always your aroma!

Loyalty and faithfulness
Reveals just how you are
In your own gentle way
You serve this church so far!

Talented and committed
Is how I see you with my eyes,
You are young, but an example
"Bless her Lord," my heart just cries!

Genuine and peaceful
Is the title you now bear
For your sacrifice of love
Is the music that we hear!

An Amazing Church Worker!

You are an amazing Servant
You light up our church world
Reflecting on your dedication
We conclude, you are a special pearl!

You are an amazing sister
You go all out for God
And so, I pause to bless you
Keep close to him like peas in pod!

You are an amazing worker
You withstood the test of time
In God's vineyard you have laboured
And you never charge a dime!

You are an amazing lady
This church thanks God for you
You are trustworthy and consistent
It keeps you fresh as the morning's dew!

Indeed, You Are Honoured!

It is indeed a blessed honour
To live a worthwhile life
You use your time to serve God
Instead of meddling about in strife!

It is indeed a wonderful privilege
To salute you on this day
For your months and years of service
We could not re-pay!

It is indeed our sweetest pleasure
To tell you how much you mean to us
For all the functions that we put on
You organize them without a fuss!

It is indeed our deepest passion
To thank and love you even more
For in your planning and your worship
Christ is the one that you adore!

A Servant of the "Most High"

You are a father to so many
From during the days of penny
We feel so safe when you're around
The wisdom you share is so profound!

You are a servant of the Most High
This fact we just could not deny
We smell the purest kind of essence
Each time you sweetly grace our presence!

You are a man of righteousness and truth
I cling to you like Naomi and Ruth
You are a part of this church's success
Because of the loving kindness you possess!

You are a blessing in so many ways
Praying, giving and encouraging all the days
This church thanks you and big you up
And Christ will always fill your cup!

You Have Been Committed!

You have been faithful, committed and true
Every day your love is fresh and new
We honour you for your dedication
In you, there is so much determination!

You have been loyal and outstanding
Quick to forgive and show understanding
I truly want the world to know
What you reap is what you sow!

You have been sowing seeds of love
As you soar to heights above
We are so proud of how you serve
Highest honours you deserve!

You have been living a life so pure
Rooted and grounded in God, I'm sure
We appreciate you for who you are
We see that God is taking you very far!

Honouring a Woman of God!

Such a mother of Zion
You're as strong as a lion
Helping us to reach a new level
You quickly kicked out the Devil!

Such a woman of God
Proudly lifting up her rod
Teaching young people how to cope
And cherish their Christian hope!

Such a child of the King
You make us shout and sing
In this church you never cease to work
You do not know how to shirk!

Such a lady of strength
You have gone to great length
To extend yourself to the call of duty
Serving God with so much beauty

Honouring a Special Lady!

You are a special Lady
You bring sunshine everywhere
For you serve God with such beauty
You are an extra-ordinaire!

You are a special Lady
Having so much love to share
For every one who knows you
Knows you always care!

You are a special Lady
You deserve a sparkling crown
You touch the lives of many
Whether things look up or down!

You are a special Lady
You have served this church so well
A long-standing and ardent worker
I just have to stand and tell!

Your Service was so Awesome!

Your service was so awesome, this we surely know
By the understanding and kindness that you show!
In Christ we are successful, as you took us from a far
"Holy and Committed" describes just how you are!

To bestow on you great honour, is why we're here today
You deserve more glorious praises, than we can ever say!
Thanks for nurturing and strengthening our souls
With dignity and grace, you fulfilled your roles!

God is your rewarder, never be dismayed
You are appreciated, for you we often prayed!
We have been impacted by the word of God you taught
And more empowered by the anointing that you brought!

You cannot be forgotten; we love you from the start
And deep within our hearts, you are the dearest part!
As a church, we salute you; keep serving at your best
The great Lord God Almighty, will surely do the rest!

You are Appreciated!

Words are not adequate
To express all I want to say
For the overwhelming blessings
You have brought my way!

But let me start by saying
You are my Beacon in the Sky
Thanks for leading me to heaven
Where no longer I will cry!

Your life is so committed
As you labour for my soul
That in Christ I am a champion
Reaching for my goal!

Today I proudly bless you
You made such difference in my life
You are appreciated
I praise God with harp and fife!

Thank you for Serving!

Thank you for serving with so much compassion
You are special; graciousness is your fashion
It is easy to love you and work with you, too
We feel your genuineness right through and through!

Godliness and grace are always on your face
Kindness and love, transcend from your embrace
We knew you were exemplary from the moment you got here
And every time you share God's word, we're floating in the air!

You will always be respected and cherished by us all
You have created memories that are standing out so tall
As fellow servants of Christ, we wish you all the best
Keep on shining; as in God you're highly blest!

As you continue to serve with humble pride
We express the gratitude our hearts cannot hide
You served with distinction, not just carry out a duty
And always displayed excellence; which reflected beauty!

You Gave Me the Foundation!

You gave me the foundation
That made me very strong
When I followed your direction
In no way I could go wrong!

You gave me the foundation
That guides my life thus far
You are competent and efficient
You are my shining star!

You gave me the foundation
That one day will make me great
For teaching me and guiding me
You are the one I appreciate!

You gave me the foundation
That makes me know myself
Talents and skills now realized
I'm no longer sitting on the shelf!

You gave me the foundation
That healed my soul so well
Out of my state of dark confusion
You lifted me; now I excel!

You gave me the foundation
That makes me stand up tall
You gave me so much hope and strength
I could not faint or fall!

Happy Retirement

With distinction, you have served this nation
With so many years of thrilling inspiration
The way you touched lives is beyond imagination
I salute you in poetry and honorary citation!

Your diligence and efficiency stand out so tall
The evidence of your work is imprinted on the wall
You are chosen of God, as far as I can recall
Today, many are inspired to carry on the ball!

You have made your mark, no part you could delete
With God as your father, there is no defeat
It was always clear; nursing is your heart-beat
If you could start all over, this path you would repeat!

As you retire, stay close to God like hand and glove
You cannot be forgotten, you gave your heart of love
You are a beautiful rose, carried on wings of dove
You must be a special angel packaged from above!

As You Enter Retirement

With remarkable integrity, you have served this nation
With so many years of heart-warming inspiration
Your willingness to serve is beyond imagination
You serve at every function in voluntary participation!

Your humility and kindness are second to none
You have the radiance of the glorious morning's sun
You are a special rose; sweeter than Easter bun
God will reward you, for all that you have done!

You have been so skilful, creative and sweet
Cooking and serving others are clearly your heart-beat
Countless Friday mornings we have the nicest treat
We often licked our fingers, at the sweetness of the meat!

As you enter retirement, keep on doing good
You will keep the peace and love in your neighbourhood
Even if others are not as kind as they always should
Never be discouraged, shine as Jesus would!

More than a Co-worker

You have been more than a co-worker
you have been mother, counsellor and friend
I will be grateful, even unto the end
your hands of love are always here to lend!

You have been more than a co-worker
When I faced my struggles and was crawling on my face
It was your kindness, that has often been my brace
The marks of your goodness, can never be erased!

You have been more than a co-worker
you have been a guiding light
For the warmness of your heart is ever shining bright
yet you keep so humbled and it feels so right!

You have been more than a co-worker
and I appreciate you so much
This is my way of saying, you have a loving touch
So glad you are Jamaican; not Spanish, French or Dutch!

-God Bless you Richly-!

A Good Samaritan

You are a good Samaritan, here is just a special token
for I want to bless you, with words never spoken
you have blessed me, in more ways than I can count
and even in your illness, with grace you keep on mount

I want the world to know, you're my guiding star
you are my guardian angel, who took me from afar
your arms of love, you daily open wide
you are the friend, in whom I can confide

When I was down and so much in need
you gladly came to help me, with your loving seed
All this time, I see you as my mother
you mean more to me, than a sister or brother

I appreciate you, and love you so much
For the kindness of your heart, and your caring touch
May God richly bless you, and preserve your health
as you keep so humbled, in challenges or wealth

A Precious Gentleman

You are a Precious gentleman
You believe in Godliness
You abide by righteous principle
And show such comeliness!

You are a Precious Gentleman
With vision and victory
You know where you are going
As you live; you make history!

You are a Precious Gentleman
You treat your lady as a queen
You set such good example
In your everyday routine!

You are a Precious Gentleman
With character pure like gold
Always so distinctive
It makes you strong and bold!

You Serve this Nation

Your journey has now come to a pause
And we stand to give you a resounding applause
It is not the end of your road
You are just setting yourself, in a more relaxing mode!

It is a privilege to serve until you retire
This means after some rest, you will refire
your labour of love, can never be in vain
Eternal blessings, I'm sure you will gain!

With pride, you serve this nation, in your humble way
you filled our lives with pleasure, more than we can say
you are appreciated, we're here to let you know
that you made a difference, in the kindness that you show!

There is no easy way, to say to you "fare well"
We are going to miss you, more than tongue can tell
your life takes on new meaning, keep leaning on that Lord
your faithful years of service, is in God's record!

Another Milestone

You have reached another milestone
Hand in hand; with God as your own
By your commitment, you are now known
Faith and love, are seeds you have sown!

You made a difference, at your work place
Despite the challenges; you often face
Like an angel, you have been our brace
You are a champion; in this life's race!

You went in full pursuit of your dreams
Motivating others, was your hobby, it seems
You sacrificed all those things that gleams
Your heart reflected such radiant beams!

You were an example, in all the things you did
Nothing good; from others, you hid
From negative people, yourself, you have rid
You were the brightest star, here, in our mid!

You are a Special Gift of God
(Dedicated to: Rev. Dr Roslyn Douglas)

You are the hand that reaches out
Amidst the thorns of life that springs about
What amazes me the most
Is how you touch lives in every coast,
I find, you are a special gift of God...!

You take the time to care and share
Your kindness is the fragrance here
Your laughter brings a special peace
that causes our pains and aches to cease
I see, you are a special gift of God...!

You must be an extra-ordinaire
Sprinkling love and beauty everywhere
You were made for a special reason
Spreading warmth in every season
I know, you are a special gift of God...!

You are the heart, that always travail
Making yourself of great avail
The strength and wisdom that you show
is the source of courage, that we know
It's clear, you are a special gift of God...!

I Want to Wash Your Feet!

The way I see you serve God
Your type is hard to beat
Your commitment is commendable
I want to wash your feet!

The way I see you love God
You're amazing and so sweet
Your service is outstanding
I want to wash your feet!

The way I see you bless God
And pray, while in your seat
You touch my heart within me
I want to wash your feet!

The way I see you trust God
And worship when we meet
It speaks so much volume
I want to wash your feet!

Chapter 2

Teachers or Preceptors

My Dear Teacher!

My Dear Teacher, you have my deepest respect
You gave your all to train me, with such good effect
Today, I proudly tell you, I thank you very much
In your eyes I see commitment; your labour is of such!

My Dear Teacher, you are the brightest star
Because your discipline is taking me afar
You are an example; in all you do and say,
With your guiding principles, how could I go astray?

My Dear Teacher, my future has been in your hands
You are moulding me, the Good Lord understands
I'll be successful, with your teaching and your tears
Selflessly you serve, all throughout these years!

My Dear Teacher, your pay comes not from man
Only God can reward you, out of his saving plan
More than a teacher; character building is your heart
Thanks for the qualities and education you impart!

You Are Most Outstanding!

You are most outstanding, this we surely know
Evidenced by the kind of commitment that you show
Today we are successful, as you helped us this far
"Generous" describes exactly how you are!

With great respect, we honour you today
You deserve more kind gestures, than we can display
Thanks for giving us a place in this institution
We are blessed by your sterling contribution!

God is your master; you serve us with kindest heart
You are appreciated; you have done your part
We will always remember, the lessons you have taught
Our lives are surely guided by the qualities you brought!

You cannot be forgotten; we love you from the start
Deep within our hearts, you are the dearest part
As students, we salute you; you're always at your best
You soar above all eagles; showing you are blessed!

My Loyal Teacher!

Thank you for training me with so much loyalty
Indeed, you are honoured, I see you as royalty
Words are not adequate, to express how I feel
For the service you give, shows your kindness is real!

What would I do without you, my teacher?
You are mother, teacher, counsellor and preacher
May God bless and keep you, as a radiant star!
And if you are ever hurting, I am never far!

Discipline and integrity characterize your personality
You are so genuine; "Jamaican" is your nationality
You are always keen in my personal development
Each day it is seen in your level of involvement!

My success today, I owe to God and you
Your kind of commitment, is found in just a few
I'll give you the roses while I have the chance
I'll celebrate your goodness, as I sing and dance!

An Excellent Form Teacher!

You are an excellent form teacher
Today this is my strongest feature
You serve with pride and joy
To teach each girl and boy!

Thank you for your labour of love
You must be an angel from above
You went beyond the call of duty
To bring out my worth and beauty!

I give you the brightest roses
For your kindness is great like Moses
Dignity and strength are your persona
Commitment and love are your aroma!

Have a Happy Teachers Day!
In this awesome month of May
To honour you, I feel so elated
You're respected and most appreciated!

You are a Wonderful Teacher!

You are a wonderful teacher
And I bless God for you
You have laid a strong foundation
This is done by just a few!

You are a wonderful teacher
You make my heart so proud
Your inspiration and your teaching
Stand out even in the crowd!

You are a wonderful teacher
Reaching each boy and girl
You go all out for children
I know you are a special pearl!

You are a wonderful teacher
There is just no one like you
Your love is always flowing
I thank and love you too!

With Distinction You Have Taught Me!

With distinction you have taught me
And I thank you so much
You understand all children
You have a special touch!

With distinction you have taught me
You are not like all the rest
You explain with greatest patience
Until each concept I digest!

With distinction you have taught me
I know God will keep you blest
With compassion and interest
You have done your best!

With distinction you have taught me
You have gone the extra mile
All students know you are effective
With your creative teaching style!

You Have Been an Outstanding Teacher!

You have been an outstanding teacher
And I'm so proud of you
You have imparted so much knowledge
I will shine in the world's best college!

You have been an outstanding teacher
making the difference in my life
The dignity with which you serve
Makes me honour you as you deserve!

You have been an outstanding teacher
You put your all in what you do
In all your students you invest
Showing deep and keen interest!

You have been an outstanding teacher
I wish you all the best
You are the most significant rose
This my heart will now expose!

Honouring My Preceptor!

My dear preceptor, I honour you with deepest respect
The type of training you gave, had such good effect
Today, I come to thank you for all that you have done
Your patience and grace helped me make a successful run!

My dear preceptor, you stand out from a far
Your teaching and guidance will take me to the star
You are an example in giving quality care
I conclude, your type is just so rare!

My dear preceptor, your greatest tools are your hands
With them you have empowered me, God understands
With you, I gained confidence in performing every task
For compensation, not one day you ever ask!

My dear preceptor, your pay from God is sure
As you help each student, I love you more and more
As for my expectations; you have exceeded them all
please accept this humble gift and place it on your wall!

"My Kind and Caring Teacher"

You have been my kind and caring teacher
Valuable lessons you always feature
So often, you go beyond the call of duty
And spread your wings for me, in such beauty!

The loyalty and commitment you displayed
ensure that my success is not delayed
The strength of your character is second to none
you always motivate me, no matter what I've done!

you are so dedicated, thoughtful, kind and true
and every morning, your love is warm and new
I salute you, on this your special day
I proudly stand to tell you; I love you in every way!

My very special teacher, I start missing you so much
I'll return to see you, and feel your caring touch
I could not repay you, for the kindness of your heart
respectfully, I tell you, in my heart you hold a special part!

"You're an Outstanding Teacher"

You're an outstanding teacher, this we have to say
Reflected in such kindness; we could not repay
Our child is successful, as you took him from afar
Words are too limited, to express just how you are!

We confer on you great honour, as we come today
For success and joy; you have brought our way.
Our child has been in this institution
Because of your love and sterling contribution

God is so amazing; he sent you with all grace
Now it is your kindness, that's flowing in this place
We will not forget the foundation you have laid
It is worth far more than all that we have paid!

You are the greatest teacher; I have ever known
Thanks for the patience; you have always shown
My family salute you; keep teaching students well
You have a heart that's golden; everyone I want to tell!

My Sunday School Teacher is Unique!

My Sunday school teacher is unique and never common
She serves with joy; no need to serve a summon
She walks with purpose and teaches us in style
While on her face, she is beaming with a smile!

Her voice is so tender, and gentle and soft
Reinforcing God's standard, she loves to do oft'
Revealing God's truth, she always does her best
And challenges us to live right when we are put to the test!

This sweet teacher, is oh so unique
Her Christian life is transparent, and never oblique
To be in her class, means our lives must be clean
God's word burns in our hearts and our liver and spleen!

She teaches so firmly and worship so hard
For she will not allow us, to get our souls marred
She teaches us to yearn for God, and cry out for more
The Lord she adores, but at the devil she roars!

My Sunday School Teacher

My Sunday school teacher is filled with lots of wisdom
She taught us the way to enter in God's great kingdom
She teaches with all of her body and soul
While God's doctrine and love, she so sweetly unfolds__

While she is teaching, her face is always beaming
For the joy of God's word in her soul is still steaming
She's filled with excitement, sweet grace and with charm
She is a true Christian, determined and warm__

Oh! I love to be in my teacher's presence
For the fragrance she wears, is God's own essence
For righteousness and holiness, is the standard she bears
And all students know that she shares and she cares__

My teacher is focused and oh, so sincere
Her passion for teaching, today, is so rare
Each day, I know that, God's on her mind
For my special teacher, is one of a kind__

My Sincere Sunday School Teacher

My Sunday school teacher prepares all through the night
She teaches her students with all of her might
She is such an amazing teacher
God's principle is her feature...

My teacher is slim, sweet and neat
And when she is teaching, she puts down her feet
This young earnest teacher is second to none
Teaching how greatly God gave us his son...

When she is teaching, we know she's sincere
For commitment and purity is the fragrance she wears
From her life I feel such virtue
when God's laws, she takes us into...

We feel passion in her teaching and see love in her eyes
Down on her knees, it's for souls that she cries
She takes pride in her teaching and pride in her life
I know that one day; someone will make her his wife...

A Rhythmic poem
"My Bible Teacher"

My bible teacher is firm; she is never bent
She teaches with her soul, and she teaches at length
She loves to teach well, and no one she resent
I love my dear teacher, who taught us how to vent

My bible teacher lives in a town called "Strident"
Whenever she drives, there is no accident
Students would go everywhere that she went
And in her behaviour, there is no form of dent

My bible teacher, must be heaven sent
For when she has taught us, we know what she meant
Oh, my dear teacher, owes no one a cent
For she taught all her students, the way to repent!

Chapter 3

God & Christianity

God is with me

God is with me, so I never walk alone
He understands my heart and thoughts
So glad to be his own
God is my dearest friend
On him I can depend...

God is with me, his presence is so real
Though "fleshly" eyes can't see him
His loving we can feel
God is a solid tower
From him, I get my power...

God is with me, his protection is so sure
And while I follow his leading
He loves me more and more
God is a refuge
So, we escape from all deluge...

God is with me, I feel safe in his embrace
No price I could repay him
For the sweetness of his grace
God is the source of love
Spreading beauty from above...

God is with me; it warms my heart so much
I would do anything
Just to feel his tender touch
God is our shield
All cares to him we yield...

All Things

All things are created beautiful
That comes from God above
All things are made wonderful
By his hands of grace and love!

All things are given freely
From the God who cares and shares
All things designed ideally
To worship without fears!

All things carved out so nicely
With thoughts of joy and peace
All things poured out precisely
To give each man a piece!

All things are moulded special
With warmth and tenderness
All things declared as equal
Having gifts and gentleness!

God's Love is so Amazing!

God's love is so amazing
It will blow your mind
If you dare to trust him
His mercy you will find!

God's love is so amazing
Reaching every man
In patience he is waiting
To show you his greatest plan!

God's love is so amazing
Regardless who you are
He will not reject you
He'll remove your sinful scar!

God's love is so amazing
Though we don't deserve his grace
When we repent, he will forgive us
And take us from disgrace!

God's love is so amazing
It will thrill your heart
In tender, loving kindness
He's with you from the start!

In Jesus

What a friend we have in Jesus
All our sins and griefs to bear__
What a joy we find in Jesus
Just to know that he is near__

What a thrill we feel in Jesus
He saved our dreadful, sinful soul__
what a privilege in Jesus
Once you repent, he makes you whole__

What a hope we have in Jesus
We have a mansion up above__
What a future, secured by Jesus
He keeps filling us with love__

What a peace we have in Jesus
all the way, it keeps us calm__
What a grace we find in Jesus
Outlined clearly in each psalm__

God is Faithful

Keep your eyes upon the mark
God will not leave you in the dark
If you don't lean on your own way
From God's love, you cannot stray!

Trust in God, for all your need
Read his word and sow good seed
Maintain his standard and stand firm
This will help you come to term!

God is faithful, don't you know?
He will guide and help you grow
Wait on him, don't run too fast
you may be haunted by your past!

Run this race, so you can win
Since you are light, without your sin
Christ bore the pain that we deserve
What a mighty God we serve!

At the Cross

At the cross I got my Ph.D.
The devil had to flee
When I got down on my knee...!

At the cross, I got my life insured
God's word I have explored
And the devil, I ignored...!

At the cross, my burdens rolled away
My night was turned to day
When Jesus taught me how to pray...!

At the cross, I gain my blessed sight
God's glory shone so bright
And now, his will is my delight...!

Only God

What do I do, when in spirit I feel so low?
Who should I ask; to restore my inward flow?
Where should I trod; so much I need to know
Only God; can renew my warmest glow!

What do I do, when I feel I cannot pray?
How should I feel, when my hair all turn to grey?
Where should I turn; when there's no sun or even ray
Only God; can give me hope for a brighter day!

What do I do, when I can't help but feel depress?
How do I cope; when my pain I can't suppress
How can I stand; when all I feel is stress
Only God; can heal and help me to express...!

What do I do, when I feel so all alone?
Where is my joy, when my meet is just the bone?
How do I connect, when I have no telephone?
Only God; cares for me while sitting on his throne!
Only God!

The Love of God

The love of God to me is pure
In rain or shine, it's always sure
It shall forever more endure
And I can't help, but cry for more!

The love of God so rich to me
He blesses me so the world can see
What could I do, to deserve such love?
That sacrifice sent through Jesus above!

The love of God, I could not earn
To submit my life; I had to learn
Only God could be God, my heart discerns
And for more of his love, my heart still yearns!

The love of God, to me is real
For in my soul, he sets his zeal
His words of love to me appeal
And all my stains and pains he heals!

God's love to me, I must adore
Out of sin, he led me through the door
He helps me with my Christian chore
Until one day, sweet heaven I tour!

Jesus Said

Jesus said, "my God, my God, why hast thou forsaken me
So that I can say, my God, my God, you have been so good to me
Jesus drank the bitter cup, so that I can drink the sweet
In the cold, he took his safety jacket off, to keep me warm beneath

Jesus said, father forgive them, they know not what they do
So that we can say, father, thanks for forgiveness,
now we know what we do
He took the lashes across his back,
so by his stripes we are healed
The spare ripped through his side,
so by his blood we are sealed

Jesus said, father, "Make them one, even as we are one"
So that we can say, through your spirit truly we are one
He was despised and rejected, so that we can be accepted
He was stripped of all defences, so that we can be defended

Jesus said, "The hour is come, glorify thy son..."
So that we can say, in the cross be my glory,
surely, through your son
He was like a root out of a dry ground,
one who assumed no beauty
Yet he pulled us out of deadness,
to show us Christian duty!

Because of the Cross

My life only matters, because of the cross
Lord, I want to tell you, of my life you are the boss
I am feasting in your word, so I can share them with the lost
Please strengthen me to serve you, no matter what's the cost!

My life would not worth anything, had it not been for the cross
I would not have potentials; I would be cold and filled with frost
Since I've been to the cross, out of my heart my sins were tossed
Help me focus on your work, rolling stone gathers no moss!

My life is of no value, without the loving cross
I have made up my mind to serve you, even to suffer loss
Jesus bore the pain and shame, and I believe I was for us
My soul was down and dreary, now, I am shining like a gloss!

I am yours

I am truly yours
I will help you do your chores
The Lord does re-assure
For us, he opens up the doors...!

Jesus, I adore
His love on us out pours
In his arms we sweetly snores
While outside, the devil roars...!

Jesus safely tours
Through my life of pain and sores
At his healing, all the people gave encores
For I know that I am yours...!

Only God Knows

I wonder where my life would be
If Jesus didn't die for me
And when my back is against the rope
How would I ever learn to cope?
Only God Knows

I wonder if I could survive
For a year, or even four or five
If Christ was not the Lord of hope
How would I stay away from dope?
Only God Knows

I wonder if I could go on
When murder, rape and strife begun
Would there be a place for me to dwell?
Outside the screams and pains of hell
Only God knows

Surely God Knows

I'm learning what life holds for me
And daily giving thanks to thee
I know I love my Lord above
And sing his praises like a dove
__Surely God knows__

I'm learning to say close to God
Even as close as peas in pod
I love to pray and seek God's way
His loving words, I will obey
__Surely God knows__

I'm learning how to stand up tall
and if I ever sustain a fall
I know he will help me quickly rise
Until I reach his paradise
__Surely God Knows__

Give it to Jesus

We give Jesus Christ the applause
For us, he died on the cross
He did it for us because
So many of us were lost...!

We give Jesus Christ all the praise
And run into his embrace
Our sinful past, he will erase
To give us a place in the human race...!

I give Jesus Christ my life
He cut away my sin, like a knife
Heal my body and soul from strife
Now I sing with a harp and a fife...!

We give Jesus Christ all the glory
When my teacher shared his story
His love can never be hoary
So, my heart will never worry...!

I give Jesus Christ my heart
In heaven, I have a part
From his love, I cannot depart
He makes me so joyful and smart...!

The Lord of Glory

If Christ was not the God of hope
How would I ever learn to cope?
If Christ was not the Lord of love
How would I get to go above?

If Christ was not the Prince of Peace
How could I learn to pray on my knees?
If Christ was not the God of Grace
How would I feel his warm embrace?

If Christ was not the saviour of the worl'
How would I walk through gates of pearl?
If Christ was not the Lord of Glory
How would I be transformed by his ever-living story?
Thank God, he is the Lord of Glory!!!

Let God

Let God's music play
To keep us in every way
Let God's music play
You don't have to go astray
Let it play!

Let God's word declare
That his coming his near
Let God's word declare
You must always be aware
Let it declare!

Let God's son save soul
To take us all out of sin
Let God's son save soul
He will make us whole
Let him save soul!

Let God's spirit anoint
To take us to the right point
Let God's spirit anoint
even our muscle and joint
Let it anoint!

Let Go and Let God

You can't solve problems on your own
Let God be your guide
And please make him known
Let go, and let God!

You can't rebel against God, and still get by
and when troubles come
You start to ask why
Let go, and let God!

You can't be effective, if you are so cold
When the devil attacks
You will never be bold
Let go, and let God!

You can't keep refusing to hear God's call
When the heat of hell pelts
You will surely start to bawl
Let go, and let God!

You can't worship God, if your soul is not well
Out of God's presence, when trial comes
Your soul, you will sell
Let go, and let God!

You can't be victorious, without God in your life
Alone, you can't overcome
Even if you are, a husband or wife
Let go, and let God!

Because Jesus knows my Name

You pierced me with your arrow
But God's eyes are on the sparrow
He knows about my tomorrow
And I'm never gonna borrow
Because Jesus knows my name__

You try to bring me down
Try to mess my name in town
But only looked like a clown
Since Jesus blesses me with a crown
Because Jesus knows my name__

You are wasting your time
Trying to make me appear as chyme
Using up every dime
When I'm filled with blessing and rhyme
Because Jesus knows my name__

Prayer

What is more effective than prayer?
To melt our hearts, and lift us hire
This is one of my deepest desire
To experience, through prayer, God's electrifying fire__

A fulfilling day, is one that starts with prayer
So, after a night of rest, one can refire
A prayerful life, is one to admire
For a committed life, God does require__

We are made whole, through worship and prayer
Knowing God is true, but the devil is a liar
From powerful prayer we cannot retire
Until we are connected by the Holy Ghost wire__

Our God

How precious and how beautiful, is our God above
How gracious and how wonderful, is our God of love
How I yearn to see him and touch his glorious face
I'm so thankful that he saved me, by his redeeming grace!

How gentle and how diligent, is our God of peace
Reaching souls in every land, even France and Greece
He is such a loving father; he takes me by my hand
So, I never walk alone, on this pilgrim's land!

How holy and how pure, is our God of light
In cleansing us, he took us, out of our sinful plight
How marvellous are the works of his creative hands
How splendid and remarkable, is our future that he plans!

How powerful and mighty, is our God of strength
How timely and completely, he cleanses us at length
How forgiving and how patient, is our God of grace
Watching us and caring for the whole human race!

My God Is

My God is Alpha and Omega, the first and the last
He is my problem solver, on him all burden's cast
He is the beginning and the ending
On him I am depending__

My God is the conquering Lion, of the tribe of Judah
Protecting and leading us to sweeter land than Beulah
He is the eternal superior being
Who, in my heart is seeing__

My God is the everlasting father, and the Prince of Peace
He sent his son to save us; his mercy cannot cease
He is a sun and a shield
All his truth to us revealed__

My God is my master and my keeper
His reward is eternal, no time to work for cheaper
See his love to us attending
While his joyous grace descending__

Loving, Gracious Jesus

Thank you, Jesus, thank you Lord!
'Tis so sweet when we're in one accord
Singing praises, with each music, with each chord
Of such moment, God keeps a record...

Loving Jesus, loving friend!
'Tis my broken heart that you have mend
Your rose of love now condescends
Oh, my Lord, what beautiful blend...

Gracious Jesus, gracious king!
To you forever, I will sing
Your words of hope, I gladly bring
to those in sin, what marvellous thing...

God is Our Source

God is the centre of all human source
To sustain life, he provides us with vital resource
It feels so good to be in his royal force
From his bond of love, there can be no divorce...

God is the central figure of all attention
Demonstrating through his son, such warm affection
In his words of hope and peace, is our reflection
as we are a part of his selection...

God is the source of all human hope
Releasing the strength, we need, to live and cope
When the future hangs on a slender rope
He grants a miracle, that surprises even the pope...!

Lord, You Are

Lord, you are my inspiration
In all I hope to be
Giving me great aspiration
Overflowing like the sea...

Lord, you took me out of deception
And helped me to receive
A seat at your reception
God's goodness to achieve...

Lord, I seek you with desperation
In my every need
Praying hard with perspiration
You are my God indeed...

Lord, each day I live in preparation
For your promising return
Reaching out to this generation
With your love inside, I burn...!

Empowered by God

I am empowered, like an eagle in the sky
God chose me for his purpose, don't even ask me why
His precious will for my life, I never could deny
He has great plans for me, so why should I defy?

This faithful God, is filling me with healing
While, with humbled heart, at his feet I'm kneeling
Since he melts my heart, his love in me I'm feeling
I want the world to know, God's love is so appealing!

God provides me with the instruments, to carry out the task
Why I'm successful, some would even dare to ask
So proud to bear his title, no need to wear a mask
He poured out his anointing, I'm loving every flask!

I see the Lord of Glory

Before Jesus touched me, I had some lonely nights
Now, I'm soaring like an eagle, reaching for great heights
I feel the wind beneath me, I see the stars above
I see the Lord of glory, smiling at me in love__

I'm flying like an eagle, glowing in the sky
Flying with great honour, to lift God's name on high
My heart feels such compassion, I know that this is real
Love expressed in every fashion, his awesome love to feel__

The radiant sun, on me is shining
To tell me, surely it is God's timing
With a clear view, I see with greater vision
To break up all division, since God took me on this mission__

God is true; he gave me re-assurance
With full coverage, he is always my insurance
With greater purpose, I seek to do his will
And while I serve him, I increase with greater skill__

God's Beauty Expressed in Nature

From the dawning of the evening
To the rising of the sun
Look at all God's goodness
See what he has done...

From the bottom of each mountain
To the top of every hill
Beholding God's creation
He said, "Occupy until" ...

From the blossom of the flowers
To the bearing of fruit trees
We gain access to God's blessing
as he handed out the keys...

From the hopping of grass hoppers
to the chirping of the bird
God's work is so amazing
as he preserves his word...

From the flowing of the rivers
to the wideness of the seas
view love in demonstration
God's beauty each man sees...

God is the Tree of Life

There is a strong tree
Deeply rooted and free
It spread its branches in beauty
So that it can be productive and fruity!

This life-giving tree
Is so wonderful to see
The branches hang caringly low
Because, from them, all blessings flow!

Its leaves are fresh and green
Having love and joy between
The fruits keep our bodies nourished
So, in good health, we have flourished!

We could not do without this tree
That cares so much for you and me
This tree sustains husband and wife
God is this tree of life!!

It was an act of Love

God sent his son to die for me
He was crucified for all to see
Christ suffered for my cruel sins
Then, a new life for me begins
It was an act of love!

He saw me, when I was all alone
With a heavy heart, I sat and moan
He passed my way to let me know
That "salvation" is the way to go
It was an act of love!

For all, he conquered death and hell
Now with his love, I run and tell
that we have to sin no more
For Jesus' blood purchased the cure
It was an act of love!

Yes, Jesus is the only one
who prepared for us, a big mansion
Regardless of the things you did
Forgiveness stood there, in your mid
It was an act of love!

Jesus loves us rich and poor
He is not partial, I am sure
My life, my love, is all for him
He lit my world, when it was dim
It was an act of love!

God Makes the Difference

God makes the difference, in relationships
It's not your face, your eyes, nor your broad hips
If you leave God out, you plan to fail
And no one can grant you bail!

Seek God's face, each day and night
Do not stray from what is right
When problems come to daunt your way
The Lord will tell you what to say!

Without the Lord, how could you live?
Who would all your sins forgive?
When so many hearts are going dim
God fills your heart, right to its brim!

Give God thanks, and praise his name
His love for us is still the same
He has placed in us, some good
To help us enjoy brotherhood!

The Earth is the Lord's and the Fullness Thereof

The earth is the Lord's, and the fullness thereof
The hills are so rocky, the seas are so rough
Stay close to God, and you won't turn a fluff
Don't stay in your corner, and huff and then puff

The earth is the Lord's and the fullness thereof
The rain is still falling, the earth is still tough
Some people complain, that there is not enough
To fill their store basket, with many a stuff

The earth is the Lord's and the fullness thereof
The grass is so tall, and the bushes are buff
Don't get in trouble, keep off the handcuff
Your tongue you should bridle, you may get a bluff

The earth is
The Lord's
And
The fullness thereof
(reptx2)

I often think of Heaven

I often think of heaven
The ultimate home for those forgiven
I can hardly wait to see what's in store
Behind the scene of heaven's door!

God has promised this place of peace
As a home of rest, for us to ease
The load of care, we have down here
Oh, what joy, with us to share!

Heaven must be a beautiful place
Designed for people of different race
My God has such a beautiful taste
We can't let this opportunity, go to waste!

Heaven is a home of eternal hope
Without which we could not cope
For when life on earth has come to an end
To which other home, could we ascend!

God is Awesome

God is gracious, kind and pure
For us, he opens heaven's door
He took away our sinfulness
And fills us with his righteousness__

God is tender, wise and true
Each day, he blesses fresh and new
I love the peace that God imparts
It keeps me safe from Satan's darts__

God is caring, great and strong
To us, he calls out "come along"
He provides for us a mansion there
To keep us far from Satan's snare__

God is awesome, nice and good
By my side, he always stood
He fills me with great songs of hope
And washed me with his cleansing soap!

The Greatest Gift of All

The greatest gift of all, was handed out to me
Purchased by my Lord, on Mount Calvary
He suffered in my place, and drank the bitter tea
This was love so free, love eternally...

The greatest gift of all, was wrapped up in God's grace
It was sealed in love, and kept in his embrace
This was for people, of all different race'
This was love so free, love eternally...

The greatest gift of all, money could not buy
To take away our sins, Jesus had to die
No other Lamb could do, none would dare to try
This was love so free, love eternally!

The greatest gift of all, is Jesus Christ my Lord
Lifting us from sin, to live in one accord
The perfect Lamb of love, has set the world record
This was love so free, love eternally!

Love that was unknown

Love that was unknown
Today, has become our own
Since in the softest tone
Jesus entered our zone
And topped up all our phone
We are never left alone!

Safely anchored in his boat
He will keep us all afloat
Christ has left for us a note
He gently took us all to vote
What a lesson that he wrote
To his work, we must devote

Nothing can go wrong
With love that is so strong
To whom do we belong?
It is not "Mr. Wong"
God said, "Come along"
He will give us a new song

Can't wait to see him face to face
He has settled all my case
My sinful past, he has erased
This is no time to waste
Heaven we can taste
To live holy, we must haste!

You Bring Out the Best in Me

I sat down to drink some tea
When the Lord took me by the sea
there, he brought me on my knee
So, he could bring out the best in me!

So grateful I'm your child, and always will be
I give all the glory, Lord to thee
You have opened up my eyes to see
That you bring out the best in me!

Caring not for my own strength
For the need of others, I go each length
God has taught me not to resent
the fact that, he will bring out the best in me!

A fresh vision today, I find
Since King Jesus is on my mind
the Lord is one of a kind
with love, he can bring out the best in me!

I May Never

As I remember Princess Diana, August, 1997

I may never enter into Buckingham Palace;
I may never be called a queen or a princess;
I may never make a famous public address;
But the Kingdom of heaven is mine;
In this my soul is truly blessed;
For life is more than food and fame;
Life is joy and righteousness!

I may never gain the world's wealth or fame;
I may never be deemed important;
But just for me Jesus came;
Surely, I will serve the Lord, because heaven is my aim;
Towards all mankind, his sweet love flows just the same;
And behold! In the King's mansion, I have a new name.

I may never sit with officials, in the house of parliament;
I may never be treated as royalty;
Nor hear a word of compliment;
But I stand to inherit the splendour of heaven;
Oh yes, my soul is confident!
So, my heart is filled with gladness, peace and contentment;
The King of Glory saved my soul, this was not an accident.

I may never walk on the red carpet,
But I will walk on streets of gold
I may never shake the queen's hand,
But my hand doth Jesus hold
When a man rejects God,
His days are few, dark, lonely and cold
The rich without God, has no joy,

If only the half should ever be told
I am an heir of the Kingdom of God,
I feel so free, strong and bold!

The Price of Blood

It was dark, lonely and very cold
When Jesus hung on the rugged cross of old
For a few pieces of silver, he was cheaply sold
His suffering was deep, the half has never yet been told!

Jesus bore the agony, terror and disgrace that I deserved
He gave his life and love for us, unreserved
We are not worthy of his sacrifice, I have observed
But he did it completely and, quite undisturbed!

He was bruised, chastised and tortured for me
He crouched beneath the sting of death, to set me free
Jesus cleansed me, so that my sins all flee
Each drop of blood was filled with compassion, I clearly see!

Thank you, Lord, I really have to cry
I can hardly believe; I cause you to die
Through the cleansing blood, you draw me nigh
Lord Jesus, between you and I,
There will always be a very close tie!

Overcome, Don't Succumb

Young people, stand up for Jesus, never you fall
Dare to make a difference, like the Apostle Paul
Press through fire, rain, wind or storm
Christ will keep you in any time, state or form...

We are gathered here in this retreat
Because we will not accept defeat
We got away from this world of deceit
Therefore, our old life of sin, we'll not repeat...

When the enemy comes in like a flood
Christ will give us the victory, through his blood
Be determined, to serve Jesus to the end
The heat is on, the storm is raging,
but on Christ, we can depend...

We are in a mighty warfare
So, on Christ, we roll our care
Respect your salvation, and be at your best
Trust in the Lord, he will do the rest...

To be strong, we must face some pressure
Our faith will certainly grow beyond measure
It is worth it all, for we will have pleasure
For heaven is the prize, we highly treasure

Jesus, is who Satan wants us to renounce
But glory, halleluiah, our lips will pronounce
Be focused, persevere, please don't succumb
Salvation is so precious, we must overcome...

God's Design

God is so unique in his design
Look at the apple, the mango and pine
Examine the flowers and distinct beauty of each kind
Just looking at nature, relaxes my mind!

God made everything perfect and fine
It thrills me to know; it's all yours and mine
We can tell each season, for we see the sign
All things were made fresh, so sacred and divine!

In the midst of the forest, the trees are refined
The colours on the lizards run in a straight line
There are herbs to cure sickness, and grapes to make wine
You are free to rest, think and even sit and dine!

The animals and plants are free, attractive and wild
Among them you can play, and just feel like a child
All your cares fade away, and you grow meek and mild
As you tell Jesus thanks, and just give him a smile!

Lord Take My Will

Lord Jesus, please take my Will
While I am humbled, yielded and still
Lord, I am sorry for being ungrateful, selfish and blind
Instead of being truly thankful and kind-

For all your blessings and goodness to me
Committed and yielded, I really should be
So often I murmur and complain
And my love and affection, from you I restrain-

I feel so ashamed, I really could die
But I must rise, 'til I reach the sweet "by and by"
I am so tired of my failures and fault
But yet Lord, it's a common assault-

Jesus, please help me calm my fears, as I wipe my tears
For I must improve, throughout the years
Control my emotion, to ease my spiritual erosion
That at last, I can give you my sincere devotion-

And thank you Lord, for taking my will,
While I am humbled, yielded and still!!!

Let Him In

Open up your heart, and let him in
He will surely cleanse you from sin
At this moment, your future seems so dim
He wants to fix things for you, only let him in!

Open up your heart, and let the saviour in
He has been waiting to make you smile and sing
Only a look at Jesus, brings you eternal life to win
He is crying out for you, only let him in!

Open up your heart, and let Jesus come in
You are battered and broken, too long it has been
He is merciful and kind, what do you think about him?
He is grieved when you ignore him, oh please, let him in!

Open up your heart, and let the Lord in
He is the only one, who can deliver you from sin
Sin is deadly, it can crush you deep within
Oh, my child, hear my voice, and let me in!

Open up your heart, and let the King of Kings come in
He will take your guilt and shame and throw them in the bin
If you insult him and reject him, hell will burn your skin
Tonight His love is still outpouring, wont you let Him in!

All the Way to Calvary

All the way to Calvary, he went for me
His love and compassion, now I can see
My heart was broken, and I bow on my knee
From that day onwards, my sins all flee__

All the way to Calvary, he went for you
Why stay in sin and become dragged down and blue?
Your sins were nailed to the cross, he cares for you too
The devil is a liar, only God's word is true__

All the way to Calvary, he went for me
Since mercy lives, he hears my plea
Can you believe, sweet love surrounds me like the sea
I am free at last, and ever more to be__

All the way to Calvary, he went for you
I thought you would cry, oh Lord, thank you!
Who will show appreciation, it's only a few
We should love Jesus, from pulpit to pew__

All the way to Calvary, he went for us
To serve him with commitment is truly a must
We gain grace, joy, salvation and plus
We are happy and blest, for in Jesus we trust__

God's Love to Man

Just like a gentle dove
God reaches down from above
And rescued man in all his love
Making our lives spicier than clove__

All his love, with us he shares
He does all this, because he cares
On the cross, agony and pain for us he bears
Can you tell me, who else dares? __

Night and day Jesus hugs me tight
And in his arms, I feel just right
He fights for my soul, with all his might
Now, to heaven, I'll take my flight__

Jesus is the greatest story ever told
His love and beauty, shines like gold
On my soul, he takes a solid fold
Just when I need his hands to hold__

Jesus loves me dearly, this I know
Because the great, holy bible tells me so
Oh, I love him too, and his praises I will show
And in his grace and beauty, I will surely grow__

Soul Winners

They know their calling, so they work
Their reward is sure, so they don't shirk
Their time and talent, is of great worth
They labour, until they sweat to their shirt!!

You're not a soul winner by what you say
Your life must be active, and firm in God's way
Otherwise, you're in bondage, or call it what you may
Exalt Jesus; he will stand by you, be it night or day!!

Working always, whether there is nothing or much
God's true people are really of such
He thrills their soul, to him they rush
Together they pray, and his pure garment they touch!!

They can't be discouraged, for in him they believe
Their motives are clean, so from him they receive
Soul winners keep pure, from sin they're relieved
Join us Christian people, and you won't be deceived!!

Dear Lord

Dear Lord, you are everything gracious, dearest and best
And when we are close, I feel sweetest and blest
In your arms Lord, let my deepest thoughts rest
And help me not to fail you, when I am put to the test!

Dear Lord, please let me be a humbled part of your heart
And Lord, I want to tell you, I love you from the start
Please take me and break me, and make me a part
Of your strong army, though at me, Satan thrust his dart!

I just want to trust you and serve you, just like I should
And be thoughtful and caring, Lord, just like you would
I yearn for compassion and tenderness, to reflect true womanhood
Let me love like you love, and be gentle and good!

Please help me bear someone's burden, and feel someone's pain
Until my heart breaks, and myself I can't contain
Then let heaven's door be opened, and pour out healing rain
That at last I'll be a blessing, and holy standards I maintain!

Lord, I Love You

You are my deepest and sweetest inspiration, dear God
Let me be warmer and closer to you, than peas in the pod
Help me fear you and love, as you rule with your rod
The meat of your word is sweeter to me than mackerel or shod
As I worshipped, you smiled at me, and in approval you nod...
Lord, I love you!

You are my gentle saviour, and my dearest friend
'Tis my heart that you have sheltered, 'tis my soul that you mend
And no one else can take your place, on you only I depend
Without you I am nothing, I will not lie about it nor pretend
God, you gave me life everlasting, and my soul you defend...
Lord, I love you!

Teach me thy ways Lord, and show me thy path
Let me be obedient and flee from thy wrath
In your grace and your blood, oh Lord, give me a bath
I want to spend time with you in fasting and prayer,
down in sackcloth
And then rise up in strength, so I can tread through life's path...
Lord, I love you!

Help me trust you completely, in my moment of need
In your word and your goodness, then let my soul feed
Show me how to wait on you, and keep my soul from greed
Let me not only love in words, but in truth and in deed
Then after all of this, may I be acceptable and daily so good seed...
Lord, I love you!

I Never Know

I never know the joy salvation brings
And that my Lord has healing in his wings
But there in my quest for earthly things
I heard the saviour say, "Search no more"
I am the King of Kings!

I never know the excitement of serving God
And that I can live close to him, like peas in the pod
But now in salvation, I keep my feet shod
And when the host of hell comes up against me
I just stretch out my rod!

I never know his divine call on my life
And that I should even be somebody's wife
But when the word of God rips through my soul like a knife
I could not help myself; I just give him my life!

I never know I could speak before a sanctified crowd
And shout the victory so very loud
And in my moments of sorrow, gloom and cloud
Jesus stepped in to say, I am with you, preach my word,
For you make me very proud!

Oh, how I Remember

Oh, how I remember, the day God saved my soul
Oh, how I remember, the day he made me whole
The memories are still fresh in me
With grace and love, he makes me what I ought to be!

Oh, how I remember, how my burdens rolled away
Oh, how I remember, when he looked at me and say
My child, I waited long for you
To bless and guide and keep you true!

Oh, how I remember, when he stamped on me his seal
Oh, how I remember, how salvation made me feel
He taught me how to watch and pray, when at his feet I kneel
God wrapped his arms around me, and filled me with his zeal!

Oh, how I remember, the first words he spoke to me
Oh, how I remember, when his kindness I could see
God showered me with love so dear
This quickly moved my doubts and fear!

Oh, how I remember, when he first took me by my hand
Oh, how I remember, when he first showed me what he planned
He took me out of deepest sins, and taught me what was right
My life, my love I give to him, his will is my delight!

God and only God

For God and only God
Can redeem us from our sins
Through Christ, the Blessed Lamb
Knowing, he always wins-

For God and only God
can help us in this life
We are in the last days
There's so much pain and strife-

For God and only God
Can give us so much hope
For in the face of chaos
He shows us how to cope-

For God and only God
Can see within our hearts
He knows the good and bad
Salvation, he imparts-

God is Forever!

God is forever and God is truth
So, truth can never die
Don't be a false witness against your neighbour
Don't even plan to lie!

God is forever and God is love
So, love you can't deny
Don't be selfish towards your neighbour
You won't be happy, even if you try!

God is forever and God is peace
So, peace you can't defy
Don't be cantankerous against your neighbour
Don't even be a spy!

God is forever and God is joy
So, joy will lift you high
Be a Godly and gracious neighbour
Only this will satisfy!

Chapter 4

Nature

Connecting with Nature

Feel healing in the rivers*
It makes my body shivers*
Feel passion in the breeze__
and it puts my mind at ease__

See beauty in the roses*
Nature's beauty now exposes*
See the freshness of the dew__
a world that is brand new__

Behold, the power of the sunshine*
Feel it warmly, from six AM 'til nine*
Behold, the glory of it too__
It helps each one, even animals at zoo__

Hear music in the raindrops*
There is good music, even when frog hops*
Hear the different sound of birds__
So, enjoy the rhythm and the words__

Smell sweet scent from the fruit trees*
As you smell them, you may sneeze*
Smell the fragrance of nectar__
Or you can enjoy them from afar__

I Wonder

I wonder why trees grow so tall
And why they lose their leaves in fall?
Without their leaves, they look so cold
But yet they keep so fresh I'm told!

I wonder where birds go in spring
And if they always love to sing
Birds always seem to stay together
In rain or shine or stormy weather!

I wonder how wild animals live
If they share preys and love to give
Animals that are eaten, must be often scared
And always wish, they could be spared!

I wonder how they feed their young
And if they ever get bees stung?
Animals must be surely clever
It seems they are here to stay forever!

I wonder why ants are so smart
And if they are so, from the start?
In sunny time, they save their food
In rainy time, enjoy good mood!

I wonder why good people die
And why those who live, would often cry?
We dare not replace them, if we try
Their works of love live on, oh my!

The Beautiful Sun

There is glory in the powerful sun
In strength and beauty, I watched it shone
It dried pimento, ginger and currant to make bun
Oh, how useful is the radiant sun!

There is wonder in the late afternoon sun
For behind the hills, it slowly runs
Just to gaze on it, I find it fun
Oh, how peaceful, is the setting sun!

There is heaven in the marvellous sun
I sought a match for it, but there was none
Making it extra special, is what God has done
Oh, how amazing, is the sparkling sun!

There is healing in the blessed sun
Restoring health in pastor, priest and catholic nun
It shoots bacteria, faster than gun
Oh, what victory, in the shining sun!

Beneath the Sea

Have you explored the ocean's floor?
All are at peace, no creatures roar
So, fascinated by the coral reef
It's a house of peace, where there's no grief!

Oh, what freedom, under the sea
A home where plants and creatures all agree
Fishes swim in fresh delight
Not one deadly shark's insight!

I saw lobsters, crabs and dolphins too
I saw sea eggs and shells, in this water zoo
There, I caught some fishes, in my net
but some jumped off, just like a jet!

It's a whole free world for us to see
A taste of heaven, beneath the sea
It's a colourful place, I can't forget
Having gone there, I can't regret!

Early in the Morning

Early in the morning, the air is fresh and clean
The beauty of the sky, the sea and earth are seen
Mountains tell the story of God's Majestic power
And the hills peak up, with radiance every hour!

Early in the morning, the sun begins to rise
With faithfulness in service, right before my eyes
God gave man the knowledge to work throughout the day
With worship songs and praises, evermore to say!

Early in the morning, birds fan out their wings
And soar beyond the mountains, how sweetly each one sings
They fly in splendid glory, as they float beneath the sky
In amazing wonder, how beautiful the fly!

Early in the morning, the trees and grass are green
As heaven kisses earth, it creates a lovely seen
What refreshing feeling, when we see the morning's dew
And feel the soft wind blowing, I love to see this view!

In the Freshness of the Morning

In the freshness of the morning,
the breeze shakes all the leaves
Telling them, "Good Morning", knowing their pet peeves
All living things adore God, and thank him for their lives
Saluting God in splendour, are husbands and their wives!

In the freshness the morning, the leaves sway in the wind
As we pray and find forgiveness, if we ever sinned
All of nature's glory, comes from one Great God
Helping us to know him, as through life, we trod!

In the freshness the morning, the trees all clap their hands
Waving, "Thank you Jesus", in words he understands
I heard the crowing rooster, and the hooting of the owls
Animals start feeding and dogs eat from their bowls!

In the freshness of the morning, I see the flowing streams
Rivers, springs and seas, are as fresh as in my dreams
In the morning's fresh aroma, I take my deepest breath
My lungs refilled with oxygen; I keep so far from death!

Very Early in the Morning

Very early in the morning
Poems rushing through my head
And in the right direction
The words now have me led!

Very early in the morning
The words just start to pour
To reach for pen and paper
I scampered through the door!

Very early in the morning
My mind is so engaged
If I don't rush to write things down
My thoughts get so deranged!

Very early in the morning
My sleep was still so sweet
But God bids me to wake up
So, I jumped out of my sheet!

Very early in the morning
Inspiration runs so free
In this place of wisdom
I'm as happy as can be!

In the Glory of the Morning

In the glory of the morning
I gazed up in the sky
The clouds were swiftly moving
As they seem to say, "Good-bye!"

In the glory of the morning
The clouds all looked so white
Spreading below the heavens
They all stretched out so right!

In the glory of the morning
The sky is fresh and blue
Separating earth from heaven
Every day the sky seems new!

In the glory of the morning
The stars faded away
The clouds and sky in splendour
In wondrous, warm array!

The Bright and Shimmering Sun

The bright and shimmering sun
Come, see all that it has done
It cures, it heals, it blesses
In amazement, it has shone!

The bright and shimmering sun
Dries my clothes on the line
The sun is my medication
It keeps my skin refine!

The bright and shimmering sun
Is all that we do need
For God in His Great Glory
Shines, in the sun, indeed!

The bright and shimmering sun
Helps us have so much fun
How could we see so clearly?
How well, would athletes run?

The bright and shimmering sun
Is dazzling through the trees
With rays that are so radiant
It brought me to my knees!

Sitting by the Stream of Life

Standing by the river side
Seeking for some place to hide
A quiet space where I can dwell
I hear no shooting, war nor yell!

Sitting by the stream of life
I keep myself away from strife
I splashed some water on my feet
And heard the sounds of my heartbeat!

Looking at the water, there
It seems so bright and crystal clear
It makes me want to take a swim
And keep so healthy, neat and trim!

Gazing with my thoughts so deep
I saw a turtle start to creep
This reminds me, God is good
For he blesses, as I stood!

God provides for each creature
He's their guide and their teacher
I love it, when I'm all alone
So much, I would not have known!

There was a River

There was a river close by my home
It was so big and clean
It was quite an amusing zone
Even birds and crabs were seen!

Looking at the water
That was so crystal clear
I wanted to dip right in it
For it seemed so fair!

While I was gazing on it
I missed my step and fell
I swam so freely in it
Its freshness I could smell!

I was not dressed for swimming
My grandma started to yell
I told her it was an accident
She was still mad, I could tell!

I did not worry too much
The river was nice and sweet
I would hug and kiss my grandma
And rub ointment on her feet!

The River

I first learn to swim in a river
It was very deep in the middle
But it was a lot of fun
I would swim, play and giggle!

It was a bathroom for many
For it was the place we often bathe
There, we also did our laundry
At the area that was swathe!

The river was a place for gathering
There's just so much we could do
It had a wonderful waterfall
Fruit trees were close by, too!

The waterfall flowed so gently
We jumped from where it starts
And when we land in the water
We swam, like we knew fine arts!

The river is still so lovely
After years have come and past
God has kept its freshness
The river was meant to last!

The Moonlight

At the dawning of the morning
I saw the bright moonlight
She was shining nicely
There to help my sight!

At the dawning of the morning
The moonlight smiled at me
I said to the moon, "Good Morning"
And watched her slowly flee!

At the dawning of the morning
The moon calls out to me
Right through my bathroom window
She was as radiant as can be!

At the dawning of the morning
The moonlight was at such peace
I gazed on all its glory
And there my joys increase!

At the dawning of the morning
The moonlight beams so right
It's always there so faithful
Shining through the night!

At the dawning of the morning
I saw the moonlight's crescent shape
Sometimes, it features as a circle
And beautify the earth's landscape!

Moonlight on the Horizon

Moonlight on the horizon
Shining brightly over the hill
It creates such a beautiful picture
It gives me such a thrill!

Moonlight on the horizon
It amazes, as it shines
So splendid and intriguing
It enlightens and refines!

Moonlight on the horizon
I love it; with all my heart
It ceases all attention
And makes everyone so smart!

Moonlight on the horizon
With grace, it shines at me
As it speaks so kind and gently
I listen and drink my tea!

Moonlight on the horizon
Complimenting sky, mountain and sea
It sits in royal splendour
It's majesty all can see!

Moonlight on the horizon
What a beauty on the hill
It charts the course for sunlight
Now fun and laughter spill!

The Stars

When I was growing up
Many stars were in the sky
Sometimes, I want to count them
Like an innocent child, I try

The stars in their galaxy
Shone so bright and fair
I learnt I could not count them
They were numberless and dear!

The stars formed so many patterns
They were such beauty to behold
Now, that they are leaving
These stars are precious gold!

These are the end of times
I wonder where star goes
The stars from heaven fall
The sky now clearly shows!

Nature Walk

Walking through the woods today
The trees are all so tall
I saw streams and rivers flowing
With one smiling waterfall!

The streams are ever flowing
The birds all sang so well
They are all so happy
As I looked, I just can tell!

As if to entertain me
The birds start flap their wings
They flew around in circle
What joy each one now brings!

Capturing the beauty
I took some pics, as well
I can make some money
As these pictures I can sell!

Nature seems to talk to me
As I spent some time alone
Everything looking at their best
I love this quiet zone!

Nature Speaks to me

When human beings are silent
Nature speaks to me
When there's no act of violence
Nature smiles at me!

The leaves and trees are dancing
As nature speaks to me
With no disturbance, only calmness
Nature winks at me!

The birds are happy and chirping
When nature speaks to me
The grass is green and lushes
As nature looks at me!

The owls would not be left out
When nature speaks to me
They flapped their wings and hooted
Then jumped right out at me!

Chapter 5

Pastors

A Faithful Pastor!

You have been a Faithful Leader
We acknowledge this so well
For you respect God's service
And deliver souls from hell!

You have been a Faithful Steward
Showing you are no ordinary man
The kind of qualities you displayed
Tells of your commitment plan!

You have been a Faithful Pastor
Preaching out of your heart of love
You represent righteousness
You were sent from God above!

You have been a Faithful Teacher
For you were called by God
With passion and with purpose
You serve him as you trod!

Pastor, you are Honoured!

Pastor, you deserve the highest honour
Because you put the Lord before
You serve with excellence and fervour
The church appreciates you more and more!

Pastor, we acknowledge your dedication
And the passion with which you have served
We pause to thank you and salute you
In God's love your family is preserved!

Pastor, we feel your loyalty and kindness
Under your ministry, we're highly blest
Behind your teaching and your preaching
Is a lot of zeal and zest!

Pastor, you are honoured for your service
As you guide us through the years
The evidence of your commitment
Is expressed in your prayers and your tears!

You Are Most Distinctive!

You are most distinctive; serving well, you never shirk
Manifested by the keenness with which you did your work
In Christ we are successful, as you helped us this far
God in his Majesty; will take you very far!

With a sense of purpose; you took this leap of faith
To take us on this journey; acting now, on what God saith
In humility; you displayed such loving ways
God's Glory shines on you, like thousands of sun-rays!

God is your advisor; he guides perfectly well
And every time we prayed; the holy power fell
Reflecting, we hold on to all Godly lessons taught
You made such a difference, his presence you have brought!

How can we forget you; who laboured for our souls
You are a man of God; with sincere and prayerful goals
Keep on walking with the Lord, his plan for you is great
Heaven now awaits you, with Angels at the gate!

Every Pastor

Every pastor is a woman or man and a half
They know how to be serious
And they know just when to laugh
They follow health protocols
And keep away Covid-19 cough!

Every pastor is a woman or man of power
They know God can be mysterious
They stay in tune with him every hour
And seek to walk upright
To make God their highest tower!

Every pastor is a woman or man of character, indeed
They don't go about feeling furious
But always sow good seed
They're a pattern of good example
God's flock they faithfully feed!

Pastor, We Have Come

Pastor, we have come to tell you thanks
Not to be false, nor to make up pranks
You are truly a man of God
With Christ, you are like peas in pod!

Pastor, we have come to say, "Well done"
You were sent by God's own son
For all you've done, we're so grateful
We can't be rebellious, nor hateful!

Pastor, we have come to make you proud
And show everyone here, in this crowd
That you have turned our lives around
And plant our feet on higher ground!

Pastor, we have come to bless you, sir
Not with gold, frankincense or myrrh
But, with hearts of love and joyful cheer
Your excellent service is so rare!

A Good Pastor Knows

A good pastor knows how to use God's gift
With joy and great gladness
Not with heaviness or madness!

A good pastor knows how to treat people
With high regards in percentage
Not as lord over God's heritage!

A good pastor knows how to use his power
With humility, grace and kindness
Not with abuse or with blindness!

A good pastor knows how to utilize time
He's in control and appreciated
Not disorganized and frustrated!

A good pastor knows how to worship God
With excitement and contentment
Not with malice, proudness and resentment!

A good pastor knows how to live life clean
At home, work, in heart and spleen
Not only when at church, he's seen!

A Pastor

A pastor often teaches about God
As God's Word is our guiding rod -
In agreement, our heads, we nod
In the gospel of peace, our feet, are shod -

A pastor is a woman or man of example
Who knows the time to serve God, is quite ample -
On his/her flock, the devil can't trample
When he has work to do, he won't ramble -

A pastor doesn't leave God's people in doubt and fears
He handles God's business like he cares -
When he preaches, many shed some tears
God's Word cuts and heals, then takes out snares -

A pastor sometimes, don't get many thanks
Some people jeer him and make up pranks -
He/she will have devotion and eat some franks
And still serve God; filling up our tanks -

The Work of a Pastor

The work of a pastor never ever stops
Even when the hand of other people drops
Each boy and girl, he lovingly adopts
So, not one of his sermons never ever flops!

The work of a pastor never, ever ends
Each broken heart, he always mends
The glory of God, a pastor transcends
His standards are firm; he never ever bends!

The work of a pastor, never completes
Over and over, God's Word, he repeats
When he preaches, the hard-core drum beats
And all the church members, send out tweets!

The work of a pastor, never finishes
When he gets home, he washes dishes
He takes care of all the fishes
And keep extending kindest wishes!

A Pastor Bears

A pastor bears great relevance
Being a woman/man or significance
You know the person is genuine, at just a glance
And not deceiving, to gain finance!

A pastor bears a heart of deep compassion
And don't just wear any type of fashion
He/she appreciates God and his creation
And makes positive impact, in the nation!

A pastor bears the agonizing pain of many
Whether or not there is no penny
He/she will never ask anyone for any
But serves God like faithful Benny!

A pastor bears good name and bad
When times are happy or times are sad
When pastors want to get so mad
God gives them strength and keeps them glad!

My Pastor

My Pastor is a God-given gift
Working for God, he moves so swift
When you're down, he gives you a lift
He guides our path, we cannot drift!

My Pastor is a blessed soul
He plays such a vital role
When he preaches, God makes us whole
We worship God, while driving toll!

My Pastor is a gracious man
He will do all he can
To reveal God's loving plan
And save souls in his life span!

My Pastor is a righteous man
He never makes anyone feels less than
He will take you in his van
He must be of a different bran!

Chapter 6

Education & Fun

Pollution

Pollution! Pollution! Pollution!
A mash up di nation (rept x 1)
Mi seh, di birds, di weeds, fishes in di seas
All are dying from water-bourne disease
So, take a stand against pollution
Cause it a mash up di nation

Pollution! Pollution! Pollution!
A mash up di nation (rept x 1)
Me seh di soap, di grease, insecticides
All are mashing up di water cites
What we gonna pass to di next generation
Since wi a mash up fi wi nation?

Pollution! Pollution! Pollution!
A mash up di nation (rept x 1)
Mineral baths, di springs, di rivers, di seas
All will keep us away from disease
So, stop all contamination
For it a cause us great botheration

Pollution! Pollution! Pollution!
A mash up di nation (rept x 2), Pollution!

DUB-POETRY
Nuh Dweet

Nuh dweet, Nuh dweet, nuh dweet, wow, wow!
Nuh dweet, nuh dweet no killing in di street
Nuh dweet, nuh dweet no weapons at yuh feet
Nuh dweet, nuh dweet no blood in di street
Nuh dweet, nuh dweet no smoking of di weed
Nuh dweet, nuh dweet if you can't hear; you feel
Nuh dweet, nuh dweet 'cause hell is real
Nuh dweet, nuh dweet no raping of the kids
Nuh dweet, nuh dweet God's spirit yuh wi grieve
Nuh dweet, yuh can't get to heaven if yuh dweet

Nuh dweet, nuh dweet a di devil's deceit
Nuh dweet, nuh dweet don't accept defeat
Nuh dweet, nuh dweet a di devil yuh fi beat
Nuh dweet, nuh dweet mind yuh can't eat meat
Nuh dweet, nuh dweet else yuh can't keep sweet
Nuh dweet, nuh dweet else yuh can't get sleep
Nuh dweet, nuh dweet mine yuh feet get weak
Nuh dweet, nuh dweet mind yuh heart stop beat
Nuh dweet, nuh dweet no killing when yuh greet
Nuh dweet, nuh dweet what yuh plan when you meet?
Nuh dweet, nuh dweet beat a hasty retreat

If yuh kill yuh can't have joy
If yuh kill yuh can't have peace
If yuh kill yuh can't have love
If yuh kill there is no hope
If yuh kill how will you cope
If yuh kill you will hang on a rope

Don't do it; Cause dat nuh sweet!
Don't do it; yuh wi burn wid heat!
Don't do it.

Mother's Cake

My mother bakes with several spice'
When she is through, cake surely taste nice
Somewhere hiding, is some kitchen mice
Waiting for some, while trying to be wise

Looking at the cakes, my eyes get beaming bright
And tasting a slice, is my warmest delight
I can hardly let them, out of my sight
As mother's cake, tastes just right

As I grow up, I'm learning to bake
For a good foundation, I cannot forsake
I dream about baking, until I'm awake
For I want to bake well, like mother's cake

When I Wake Up in the Morning

When I wake up in the morning
Poems fill my mind
I wanted more sleep
So, I covered up in bed!

When I wake up in the morning
The Lord spoke to me and said:
Write down the words I gave you
To help a newly-wed!

When I wake up in the morning
These words I wrote and read:
Jesus cares about you
So, seek my face instead!

When I wake up in the morning
I praise God and spread my bed
Then quickly fold my blanket
It was fluffy, warm and red!

Culture

Culture is so different
In various parts of the world –
We operate within our culture
Whether our hair is straight or curled –

We are all influenced by culture
It helps to shape our social norms –
We function within this framework
Reflecting on the friendship each one forms –

Sometimes, we get culture shock
When we travel to different places –
Things are just not done the same
We confirm this with our faces –

The things we do in our home town
We can't do them elsewhere, as we like –
We must adjust our thoughts and feelings
And adapt and use our psyche –

The Bathroom

The bathroom is sometimes the smallest place
Providing us with the most private space
So that we can come face to face
With the need to get rid of our toxic waste

When hungry, the bathroom is the most insignificant place
But when full, it becomes the most needed space
A place where we feel no disgrace
To rid our bodies of bulk and air, while on the base

A house is not complete, without the bathroom place
Where we wash our sweaty bodies and face
We could never do without the bathroom space
Whatever is our need, the bathroom solves each private case

A Bathroom well cleaned and kept

A bathroom that is well cleaned and kept
Is a bathroom that is often swept
For dust and dirt, in it not left
Is a bathroom well cleaned and kept

A bathroom that is well cleaned and kept
Is one in which, we often slept
For the parts there in, we owe no debt
It is a bathroom, well cleaned and kept

A bathroom that is well cleaned and kept
is one in which, we often prayed and wept
For it is often safe from theft
It is a bathroom, well cleaned and kept

The Gate to a Home

The gate to home provides security
It serves us with so much surety
So firmly, a gate stands in its place
From robbers and thieves, it acts as a brace...

The gate to a home, is strongly built
With materials far stronger than clay or silt
A gate adds so much beauty
And never fail to do its duty...

The gate to a home, enhances privacy
And bears great primacy
It may or may not have an alarm
But does its part, to keep us safe from harm...!

The Living Room

The living room says, can you see me?
How greater can my beauty be
Visitors are welcomed in
But not allowed to practice sin...

The living room is set to entertain
A place for our goals and dreams to ascertain
There, love and friendship are sweetly cherished
But misery and strife are quickly perished...

The living room is such a marvellous place
Where loving hearts and arms embrace
Fun and laughter fills the air
So often too, we worship there...

Appreciate Health

One must learn to appreciate health
It is far greater than gold or wealth
Without good heath, we cannot live
A qualitative life, to serve and give

To have good heath, should be our goal
Before we can play our national role
It is good heath that makes us feel
Compassion to see our sick ones heal

Without good health, we cannot produce
Export and revenue, will start reduce
How will our people learn to cope?
Unless in God, they put their hope

This island is our happy home
From it, we will not ever dare to roam
Today, we pray for health and love
So, we can surely soar above

Despite the economic world downturn
When failing hearts all start to burn
With health and love, Jamaica will earn
A rewarding harvest, in return!!!

That Child

Reach that child, so far
He will not stay lost
help him be a star
regardless of the cost!

Touch that child around you
And squeeze him, oh, so tight
Give him a place beside you
Fill him with warm delight!

Bless that child outside
And treat him as your own
Give him a place inside
He will praise you, when he's grown!

Love that child out there
Though he seems so wild
Your love will draw him near
'till he gets tender, meek and mild!

My Easter Bun

As I sat outdoor, to eat my Easter bun
Jealously, I was slapped by the sun
Then sweetly, kissed by the wind
Frozen by the moment, on my seat I was pinned.

The upset sky, was quickly getting dark
The clouds shouted, "You should disembark"
and soon, I was showered by the rain
In my heart, I wanted to remain.

As I got up, to rush indoors
"Run faster," the incessant rain implores
I was hindered by the breeze
So, soaking wet, my clothes I had to squeeze.

My bun was in a mess
I felt a little stress
It was really sogging wet
Feeling like a fish, caught in a net!

Teach a Child

Teach a child to live
And show him how to give
Teach a child to laugh
Help him write a paragraph

Teach a child to love
And tell him not to shove
Teach a child to learn
And you will help him earn

Teach a child, to forgive
And you will help him live
Teach a child to rise
To reach to paradise

Teach a child, to believe
And from God, he will receive
Teach a child to achieve
And he will never leave.

Jesus a mi Greatest Hero

Mi Hero, mi hero, mi hero
A Jesus a mi greatest hero (rept x2)
Mi seh, mi love Bustamante
An mi love Sam Sharpe
Mi love Paul Bogle
An mi love mi Nanny
Dem fought very hard, for mi social freedom
But Jesus fought for me total freedom!

Mi hero, mi hero, mi hero
A Jesus a mi greatest hero (rept x 2)
Without di hero, yuh life it a zero
Without di hero, yuh dead like Nero
Freedom, freedom, a Jesus gi mi fi mi freedom (rept x 2)
A Jesus a lead mi to di Kingdom
A Jesus fill mi wid wisdom

Mi seh, mi love George Gordon
an mi love Garvey
Mi love Manley
An mi love mi Nanny
Dem fought very hard fah mi national freedom
But Jesus fought fah mi spiritual freedom (rept x 2)

Jamaica...to the World

I feel as fresh as a young beautiful bride
with my heart filled with so much national pride!
We have footballers and cricketers
Our nation's name is known to the world__

I saw my Jamaica, at the front page
reflecting victory, at the world's stage!
We have volley ballers and sprinters
creating history, now to the world__

Our athletes put Jamaica on the world map
Good training and discipline are what they adapt
We have net ballers and tennis players
winning gold medals, wow! to the world__

Our little island is right on top
From all over the world, tourists make a stop
Good music, food and fun, we have featured
Jamaicans, send a big "shout out," right now to the world__

This marvellous island shining bright
With sparkling sunshine beaming right
White crystal sand beaches tossing their waves
Saluting our people, as they shine right now, to the world__

JAMAICA

Jamaica is a gracious nation
With people of great aspiration
Athletes find it a training station
Since it provides so much inspiration!

Jamaica is a beautiful nation
Our national dish is a good combination
The colours of the flag are for adoration
This culture is loved by the next generation!

Jamaica is a peaceful nation
Its people show kind consideration
And in sports, have sweet anticipation
That we'll shine, with each participation!

Jamaica is a strong and free nation
We cast down wrath and indignation
We thrive hard with much perspiration
To build a firm and true foundation!

WHAT A PROUD NATION!!!

Its name is Money

We work so hard for it
Without which we all will quit
To get more, we must wait a bit
Its name is money!

Without it, we feel so stressed
With it we feel so blest
We need it from the east to the west
Its name is money!

We need it for almost everything
To the shop, it we must bring
We need it to put on a ring
Its name is money!

It makes good friendship ends
It makes some marriage mends
It some people will lend
Its name is money!

When I Have Money

I have so many friends, when I have money
It fills my house with so much honey
I feel so good when I have money
It makes the weather around me sunny-

I have comfort, when I have money
It makes me hug and love my Bunny
I am so thrilled when I have money
It makes me laugh at jokes, not funny-

So relieved, when I have money
My heart beat becomes less runny
So "frightened," when I have money
I run to the shop, and soon I "done it"!!

There's no day like Pay Day

On this special, happy day
I work as hard, as I may
So thankful, I can say
There's no day, like pay day!

In a nice and loving way
I go to collect my pay
So grateful, I can pray
There's no day like pay day!

With joy and peace, I sign
because, this money is mine
I rushed, to work on time
because, there's no day like pay day!

I burst with excitement
and eat with enjoyment
glad, to be independent
oh, there's no day like pay day!

Dub-Poetry
(In Jamaica Creole Language)
"Just in Time"

Jesus save' mi, just in time
Just when mi life a drop off a line
Mi nearly kill mi self, wid di rum and di wine
But Jesus save' mi, just in time.

Jesus save' mi, just in time
Just when mi mout' was filled with grime
Now mi feeling so refine
Fah Jesus save' mi, just in time.

Jesus save' mi, just in time
Just when a start to mix wid crime
Mercy meet mi auh show mi a sign
When Jesus save' mi, just in time.

Jesus save' mi, just in time
Just when mi heart was sour like lime
Now mi mout' it full up a rhyme
Fah Jesus save' mi, just in time.

Jesus save' mi, just in time
Just when mi teef, auh nutten was mine
All mi did have, was an apple an a pine
But Jesus save' mi, just in time...Ayayi!

Dub-Poetry
"Just in Time"

Jesus saved me, just in time
Just when my life was dropping off line
I nearly killed myself, with the rum and the wine
But Jesus saved me, just in time.

Jesus saved me, just in time
Just when my mouth was filled with grime
Now I'm feeling so refine
For Jesus saved me, just in time.

Jesus saved me, just in time
Just when I started to mix with crime
Mercy met me and showed me a sign
When Jesus saved me, just in time.

Jesus saved me, just in time
Just when my heart was sour like lime
Now my mouth is filled with rhyme
Because Jesus saved me, just in time.

Jesus saved me just in time
Just when I stole and nothing was mine
All I had was an apple and a pine
But Jesus saved me, just in time...

Ayayi!

NURSERY RHYME
I Love You Dad

Hey, hey, hey __ I love you dad
Hey, hey, hey __ with you, I'm always glad

Hey, hey, hey __ I love you dad
Hey, hey, hey __ without you, I'd be mad

Stay, stay, stay __ I love you dad
Stay, stay, stay __ when you're gone, I'm very sad

Stay, stay, stay __ I love you dad
Stay, stay, stay __ you're the best friend I've ever had

Say, say, say __ I say, I love you dad
Say, say, say __ I am your little lad

Say, say, say __ yes, I love you dad
Say, say, say __ I am good, I'm never bad.

I love you, dad

POEMS

Poems are more than rhyming words
They convey the songs of joyful birds...

Poems are more than memory gems
It's the warmth and peace that grace transcends...

Poems are more than tinkling sounds
It's the story of life's ups and downs...

Poems are more than feelings
They foster many inward healings...

Poems are more than matching lines
They speak the language, the heart designs...

Poems are more than rhythms
They sing the songs of joyous hymns...

Poems are more than words impart
They are true reflections of the heart...

So, read them over from the start!

It's Curry!

My mother cooks the nicest curry
When she's in the kitchen; no need to worry
Can't wait to eat some; I'm in a hurry
Don't even want to share it; friends I'm sorry!

The essence of the pimento, seasoning and ginger
Cause all visitors to sit back and linger
When you get a plate; you must lick a finger
It will make you addicted; just like a binger!

The curry colour looks so bright and rich
Your eyes run water and started to itch
I eat it every day; just can't make a switch
It had me in a daze; I fell in the ditch!

My mother has such an awesome taste
The gravy simmer down to the perfect paste
When it is ready; we're all in a haste
To eat it all off; not a drop we waste!

DUB-SECTION
Curry nice, curry rice, curry with spice
Curry meat, curry heat, curry so sweet
Curry gold, curry old, you were told
Curry goat, curry vote, run a curry boat
Curry right, curry site, curry at night!
IT'S CURRY!

You

You are serving happily
God has blessed your family
No one can treat you shabbily
You are genuine and not hammily!

You can never get lonely
Though you are so homely
Jesus, you worship, only
As you lye so pronely!

You are ever so chirpy
And after eating, burpy
Every year you go to Turkey
Although the plane gets jerky!

Your face is always smiling
You wear clothes of awesome styling
Money, you were always piling
To bless others; not just profiling!

Dear Dad, Dear Mom

Dear dad, dear mom, your love I'll keep
With God and you, I sweetly sleep
No cares, no tears my heart to beep
With you I'm safe, no cause to weep!

Dear dad, dear mom, I tell you this
When I think of you, I feel such bliss
All the pampering, I truly miss
I blow to you, a daughter's kiss!

Dear dad, dear mom, this you must know
Your caring, kindness helped me grow
So, in God's grace I sweetly glow
Now, Praise and Worship is my flow!

Dear dad, dear mom, I'm not my own
God leads my life, while on his throne
Not one day, I walk alone
God talks to me in a loving tone!

Dear dad, dear mom, thank you this day
You guided me in a loving way
I would be ungrateful not to say
You're the greatest parents, I shout, yay!

How Can Someone Hurt a New-born?

How can someone hurt a new-born?
And scream at them, like tooting horn
They're often wet from night 'til morn
Give them milk, not roasted corn!

How can anyone hurt a child?
How could you let them be defiled?
You are deceived and so beguiled
I pray you will now be exiled!

How can people hurt young kids?
If you destroy them, God forbids
Watch over them; use your eyelids
We want to see our great grandkids!

How can humans hurt children?
They are gifts from God, so treat them well
In arms of love, let children dwell
Let them grow and start excel!

The Kitchen

A house without a kitchen
Is one so incomplete
For there would be no place
To cook the food, we eat!

The kitchen adds such beauty
There, within my house
Creating so much warmness
Among my family and my spouse!

I love this blessed kitchen
For in it, I learn to cook
Nothing there is wasted
Not even one small nook!

Thank God for my kitchen
In faithfulness it serves
There to feed so many
As each person, so deserves!

Words of Wisdom

A house without a man
Is like a kitchen without a knife
And a man without his wife
Is like a man without his life!

A child without a parent
Is like a child without a head
And a parent now misled
Is like a parent who is dead!

A car without a driver
Is like a car you disapprove
a drunken driver you remove
is like a man that cannot move!

A church without a pastor
Is like building without a plan
And a plan without a man
Is like a drunkard in his van!

A class without a teacher
Is a class of gross disorder
Teaching without order
Is like a broken tape recorder!

How Can Anybody Hurt Our Teens?

How can anybody hurt our teens?
Don't they know what all this means
We're destroying our very own genes
Who will be our kings and queens!

How can anybody hurt our teens?
Damaging their liver and spleens
Some don't live until nineteen
We want to see our sweet "sixteens"!

How can anybody hurt our teens?
Around our young ones, put some screens
Protect our youths; give them vaccines
Give them vegetable soup and beans!

How can anybody hurt our teens?
They are as delicate as sardines
A hateful, hurtful word demeans
Support them in front and behind the scenes!

You Were an Average Student!

You were an average student
But you work hard to reach the top
For you wasted no time
Not even one small drop!

You were an average student
But you focused on your work
You have refused bad company
Determined not to be a jerk!

You were an average student
Teachers didn't think too much of you
But you persevere through trials
And God gave you great I.Q!

You were and average student
But, not one day you ever shirk
In the bank of Nova Scotia
You were the greatest clerk !

You were an average student
But you have an ambitious mind
Today, you are a teacher
Proving you are one of a kind!

Silly Billy Goat

I have a silly Billy goat
He used his horn and broke my boat
And then pulled down my aunt's petticoat
My life jackets now start float!

I have a silly Billy goat
In his mouth, he took the remote
As if he wants to promote
All the TV shows, I wrote!

I have a silly Billy goat
He tore up my love note
To keep him calm, I have antidote
But, how do I get it pass his throat!

I have a silly Billy goat
I want to sell him, I'm writing a quote
Where should I send him, help me vote
To this goat, so much I devote!

My Thoughts

As I wrote and think
My pen ran out of ink
My thoughts began to sink
And my right eye made a wink!

As I searched for another pen
My thoughts start flowing again
I found it there, that's when
I heard my crowing hen!

I sat back down to write
My thoughts were all so bright
With vision and insight
I wrote all through the night!

Writing Poems

Sitting in the woods
I leaned back on a tree
There, in meditation
Sweet thoughts came to me!

The words were always flowing
My thoughts were all so fresh
Captured by the moment
With nature, I just mesh!

To write the words was easy
My background music was the streams
The words were also rhyming
Far beyond my dreams!

After writing poems
I felt so satisfied
With pen ink that was flowing
I could not be denied!

Good Families

Good families are well organized
As they work together, everything synchronized
When they performed duties, they harmonized
It makes them relaxed and seem hypnotized!

Good families are refreshing; they seem deodorized
Thoughts of gratitude they keep memorized
The things they planned, always materialized
Then sweet success, each one realized!

Good families do things unique and specialized
No task undone; everything finalized
They speak their minds; everything verbalized
The importance of character has been emphasized!

Good families are stable and regularized
They're never indifferent or destabilized
No one in the house feels demoralized
Each person's ability is well recognized!

Good families worship God together and feel mesmerized
As they surrender all, they are energized
They don't do things without being authorized
And never leave a young child unsupervised!

Watch Your Mental Health!

You spend so much time
Accumulating wealth
Why don't you start
Look after your health!

Without mental health
You can't get wealth
You're always moving
In the mode of stealth!

With pangs and pain
Many hearts start melt
With the issues of the mind
You have not dealt!

When problems come
And sun start pelt
You jumped out your mind
And took off your belt!

Without mental health
You have not felt
That on your knees
You should have knelt!

Health or wealth
Look after your health
Health or wealth
Watch your mental health
Health or wealth
With which you've dealt!

Beauty is

Beauty is temporary
But character is lasting
So, let's build ourselves
On prayer and fasting!

Beauty is fading
But integrity is forever
Living by God's Word
Makes us warm and clever!

Beauty is passing
But reputation will stay
Dare to live holy
And do as God say!

Beauty is short-lived
It's often deceiving
What comes from the heart
You may find unbelieving1

Beauty is leaving
No time for delay
We put emphasis on it
But it goes all away!

Mental Health

Mental illness is often stigmatized
Leaving sick people traumatized
Smoking leaves you broke and pauperized
And brings you to the grave, before you realize!

Mental health is better when you exercise
Eat good food and never compromise
If you lose your mind, you may be ostracized
And even if you live, you're just marginalized!

Mental health keeps you happy and free
And when you meditate, it's just God you see
When trouble comes to sting you, just like a bee
Just cry out to Jesus, down on your knee!

Mental health holds the key to your life
Whether you're a boy, girl, husband or wife
Smoking and drinking cut like a knife
And plunge you in darkness, trouble and strife!

Ring-a-ling-a
Ring-a-ling-a
Mental Health x 3

Good mental health will bring you to your wealth x 2
There is social health and financial health
There is physical health and economical health
But Mental Health
Is the greatest health

Shades of Beauty

Some persons beauty jumps out at you
While others are a bit concealed
There are different shades of beauty
See which one is now revealed!

Beauty can be captivating
But do we handle it well
Some persons flaunt their beauty
And charm you with their spell!

Beauty shines within its season
It amazes and intrigues
But when its glory passes
It's disheartening and fatigues!

What kind of beauty is more important?
Is it the one that's just skin deep?
Beauty with good character
Keeps on shining when you sleep!

Sometimes beauty is so obvious
Other times you have to look so keen
Whether it appears quickly or more slowly
Beauty is always seen!

There are different shades of beauty
It has more colours than we think
Beauty is not just outward
When you see it, smile and wink!

Beauty

Beauty is not silent
It always speaks so loudly
With words so strong, yet tender
It lifts your heart so proudly!

Beauty is forever
Though the physical one may fade
Handle it with dignity
And it will always be displayed!

Beauty expressed in kindness
Is perfectly arrayed
It starts within its boundary
Endless beauty God has made!

Beauty with character
Is one so well controlled
In a person so qualitative
Is a treasure made of gold!

When you find yourself with beauty?
Give God all the praise
Don't flirt around so cheaply
Respect yourself always!

What's Behind that Beauty?

You are looking so bright and beautiful
But so much persons wear a mask
Beyond the realms of outward beauty
God knows your secret task
So, tell me, what's behind that beauty?

Skin so smooth and hair well done
You're a beautiful sight to see
But behind your front appearance
Are you as genuine as can be?
I wonder, what's behind that beauty!

You are always well coordinated
Your trend and style are nice
But how will that beauty matters
If you're not honest and precise
Show me, what's behind that beauty?

Your eyes are eyes of jasper
Your shape is so unique
You seem to have it all together
But are your qualities transparent, or oblique?
Can I see, what's behind that beauty?

If you have nothing, but outward beauty
No character, self-worth or pride
You may not use your full potentials
Your self-esteem and abilities hide
Do you know, what's behind that beauty?

It is sad, if all you have is
beauty
For it may cause an unpleas-
ant surprise
Beauty with purpose, makes
one successful
Your lips hypnotize; your hips
mesmerize
But, what's behind that
beauty?

There's a Busy & Bustling Market Place!

There's a busy and bustling market place
So much going on; it needs a new face
It helps many people in the human race
Yet, sometimes it is a disgrace!

There's busy and bustling market place
To shop down there, you need some grace
Everybody going at their own pace
With graffiti, some even dare to deface!

There's a busy and bustling market place
Everywhere you go, some robbers chase
If you put down your bag, to give an embrace
It will be snatched in front your face!

There's a busy and bustling market place
So crowded, there's no breathing space
The authorities can't even handle the case
All the thieves we hastily want to erase!

My Engagement Party

My engagement party was such refreshment
From the clock ticked off, at the commencement
I looked through eyes of bright discernment
And saw no one who had resentment!

The day was filled with excitement
With joy, peace and enjoyment
No one thought about employment
The air had freedom; no torment!

We had endless entertainment
There was no form of mismanagement
When it was time for the announcement
Everyone listened to the pronouncement!

The day went well; without disappointment
It was a day of love and recommitment
Friends gave support and endorsement
In a season of friendship embracement!

Chapter 7

Motivation Inspiration Encouragement

The Gift is Inside of You!

There's a gift from God in every man
From foundation you were in his plan
Trust his plan, do what you can
Stop looking left and looking right
The gift is inside of you!

Why grumble about your type of gift
Be thankful and start moving swift
Gifts not used will always drift
Stop murmuring and complaining
The gift is inside of you!

Are you wondering what your giftings are?
And whether or not you can go far
Wishing you were a famous star
Stop gazing on what others have
The gift is inside of you!

God is not partial, nor unfair
He has given each man a share
Of his grace and love my dear
Stop and reflect a while
The gift is inside of you!

"The gift is inside of you, oh yes, the gift is inside of you
And you, the gift is inside of you and you
The gift is inside of you, it's true
The gift is inside of you
Thank you"

There is Something Intriguing About Prayer!

There is something intriguing about prayer
Without it our souls become like clothes in a spin dryer
Then we become useless like a worn-out car tyre
In the field of life; better let God be your umpire!

There is something intriguing about prayer
It resurrects us from the dead and the quagmire
New life springs up in us with zeal to inspire
We sing and shout praises with the heavenly choir!

There is something intriguing about prayer
It connects you with God, like current in a live wire
All dross burnt out like fat in a deep fryer
And soon you're filled with Godly desire!

There is something intriguing about prayer
It purifies the soul like gold in fire
Then behoves us to worship God and lift Jesus higher
And spread the gospel louder than a town crier!

There is something intriguing about prayer
It relieves the soul from the mock and the mire
Oh God, thank you Jesus, we escape hell-fire
Representing heaven; we wear royal attire!

There is something intriguing about prayer
It propels us to surrender, heal and aspire
And make us emblems the world can admire
Love God and do his will is all that he requires!

There's a Life

There's a life that's filled with meaning
When you trust the hand of God
There's a life that's filled with purpose
If where he leads you; there you trod—

There's a life that's filled with beauty
Where its glory never fades
There's a life of sweetest splendour
It flourishes and it shades—

There's a life of God's own glory
His wonders to unfold
There's a life with his agenda
His people he has told—

There's a life that's filled with wonder
Of God's majesty and his love
There's a life of great fulfilment
When we honour our God above—

There's a life of God's own nature
His loving he reveals
There's a life in God's galaxy
His aesthetics now appeals—

If You

If you stay faithful to God
While climbing up your mountain__
He will pour out his great blessing
It will flow just like a fountain__

If you truly worship God
even when you are in need__
you will soon find out
that in all things you will succeed__

If you wait in patience
your hidden blessings of today__
will be revealed tomorrow
in God's own special way__

If you are thankful for small mercies
You will see that God is good__
He will then open greater doors
He's faithful, this must be understood__

Don't be Fooled

Money can't buy my eternal soul
No one else can fulfil my role
No matter what I gain in life
Without God, I'd be in misery and strife!

When I reach the end of my rope
Only God himself can help me cope
Money and fame, can get me blind
And when God comes, I'm left behind!

Don't be fooled by what you see
For beautiful heaven is the place to be
If you get trapped by riches on earth
You may never know what your soul is worth!

So, let's put God first in our lives
Boy, girl, parents, husband or wives
The mouth of hell always enlarges
To swallow more people as it engorges!

We're Strong

You will always be my husband
In sickness and in health__
I will always be your darling
In poverty or wealth__

I will be here for you
Regardless of the price__
for with Jesus, we can make it
In his love, we feel so nice__

Life is not without some problems
But we can work it out__
Faith and peach we embrace
Instead of fear and doubt__

With your smile, I am inspired
In your arms I do belong__
I am learning how to dream big
Despite challenges, we're strong__

Underneath your Belt

People like you are honoured with the broad belt of power
It signifies authority and victory every hour
With dignity you lead, and what joy you must have felt
When you defended your title, then behold
What's underneath your belt!

You must be outstanding, to wear that broad belt of honour
you are the champion, reigning with such vigour
you brought encouragement, when hearts started to melt
With God you made the difference, with that thing
Underneath your belt!

It is humbling, but yet great, sitting in such chair
For loyalty and faith, is in the broad belt that you wear
you always pray for people, while on your knees you knelt
To keep your strength alive, hold on tight to love
it's underneath your belt!

You have the courage of a hero, you are royal, brave and strong
With your charisma and your style, surely nothing can go wrong
Keep shining like a star, though rain may fall or even pelt
Just reach down and touch that armour that is
Underneath your belt!

What Will Become of Our World Tomorrow?

What will become of our world tomorrow?
When today all some feel, is so much sorrow
With the jobs we lost, and high rise in fuel cost
There is a need to care and share, for in these trial times we must!

What will become of our world tomorrow?
When today all some see, is so much horror
With often failing health and wealth, some people worried hearts will melt
There is a need to know the saviour, for with my heart the lord has dealt!

What will become of our world tomorrow?
When today all some do, is always borrow
With so many kids to school, and increasing cost of food
There is a need to pray together, to keep us from depressive mood!

What will become of our world tomorrow?
When today all some have, are visions that are getting narrow
With this financial world downturn, and overwhelming hearts concern
There is a need for passion, to help someone know how to earn!

What will become of our world tomorrow?
When today some don't know, God's eyes are on the sparrow
With this in mind, I will be kind, in any way I can
There is a need to read God's word, for in them is his plan!

Reality Check

Smoking may cause pleural effusion
While the mind gets lost in utter confusion
Every day you wake up in deep delusion
And find yourself in dark seclusion!

Everything should be used in moderation
Lest you lose control and cause botheration
The police carry out sting operation
Next thing, you drop out of the population!

We're tired of wars and aggravation
We want to have peace, in our little nation
In God's Word, there's revelation
Not only hope and inspiration!

Jump out of sin, receive salvation
Aren't you weary of degradation?
Overcome the devil and temptation
Start a new life and declaration!

Cry out to God, join the congregation
You will get support and consolation
And form clean thoughts of meditation
To lead a life of love and reputation!

Ability in Everyone

God has given everyone the ability to get wealth
It is his will that we all stay in health
God is not partial; he deals with us fair
He carves out our future, and he'll guide us there!

God deals with each man, according to his ability
To establish in his life resounding stability
Man, sometimes stray, and form his own affinity
But God gives man a chance to turn to divinity

Embedded in each man, is a raw natural talent
Develop on it, and at challenge don't relent
You can't hide your talent and bury it, too
Use what you have, else you cannot be true

God made it possible, for us to reach the star
For his gracious presence, from us is never far
Listen closely, for he gives us clear direction
For only in sweet Jesus, is our only true protection

Everyone

Everyone needs love and affection
Even if you're mentally ill –
No one should be treated lightly
As we journey up life's hill –

Everyone is a someone
And came by someone's belly pain –
Therefore, it is our duty
Not to treat them with disdain –

Everyone needs a chance in life
So, show some love today –
Do whatever you can
In the kindest way –

Everyone needs a shoulder to lean on
Sometimes we need support –
Let's give a helping hand
And please do not extort –

Everyone needs to feel a part of
So, don't ignore their need –
When it is in your power
Be sure to do good deed –

The Work Place

The workplace can be a warm, happy and compassion place
With people from various different race
Bonding together, and working as a team
Achieving so much daily, it feels like a dream!

In laughter and fun, we will work in the sun
Until every drop of our work, we have graciously done
We feel joyful and grateful, for the lives we have touched
We look forward to work; on our jobs we stay clutched!

Being at the workplace means I see various face
While I work for my living, there can be no disgrace
Each day I learn more, and it makes me feel sure
That for each person's problem I hand out the cure!

Oh! I am fascinated with my sweet work place
For with my co-workers, God's love we embrace
So, at the end of our day, we don't feel like a wreck
And at the end of the month, we do take home a cheque!

Self Esteem

It's great to have good self-esteem
You will climb mountains, no matter how high they seem
There is no limit, to what you can achieve
As long as in your heart, this is what you believe!

Good self-esteem will push you to the top
And to listen to negative people, you cannot even stop
It gives you the confidence, to go sweetly on
Before long, you will know, the battle you have won

The world will salute your success
If good relationships, you always harness
Good self-esteem, will keep your dreams alive
Just be humble, one day soon, you will arrive!

Believe in yourself...Reach for the stars

Believe in yourself, believe in your dreams
Believe in God, for your soul he redeems
Pursue all your dreams, pursue all your goals
Do your research, until all information unfolds....

Be at your best, though Satan tries to test
Trust in God all the way, your soul will be at rest
Be true to yourself; be true to your friends
Let grace and peace transcends, 'till all your trial ends....

Dare to be a Daniel, dare to stand alone
Dare to eat sweet chicken meat, and dare to eat the bone
You will triumph against the odds, you will hit sweet spotlight
God will come through the clouds for you, whether day or night

Use your talents, your abilities and potentials
Then and only then, you will gain all your credentials
Don't listen to your fears, and wipe away your tears
God will give you all the gears, so you can make it through the years

Fight with all your might, fight for what is right
Always keep your focus, never lose your sight
Some days, in your mind, there may be some type of wars
But, while some aim for fancy cars, you just, reach for the stars.

Just be humble, just be still

Just be humbled, just be still
Take your time climb up the hill
If you grumble, if you kill
You will stray from God's own will!

Just be humbled, just be still
Please be safe and close the grill
If you're grumpy, like old Bill
You will never keep your skill!

Just be humbled, just be still
Won't you stay like Sister Jill?
If your stomach gets too fill
You will surely start to spill!

Just be humbled, just be still
Just stop grinding at the mill
Since you would not take your pill
You may become a big fat nil!

Just be humbled, just be still
Keep good friends, and learn to chill
Trust in God, and work until
Your sweet soul, he starts to thrill!

Learn to Forgive

The way to be free, is to learn to forgive
Only, when you forgive, you really start to live
Refusing to forgive leaves you bitter and cold
Before you realize, you will be getting old...

The way to be healed, is to learn to forgive
For if we don't forgive, true love we cannot give
Holding on to hurts, will keep you stuck in your past
While the world passes you by, and in hell your soul is cast...

The way to be real, is to learn to forgive
Those who don't forgive, lose their lives through a sieve
Without forgiveness, you're bound to be false
Empty your heart, so you can hear when God calls...

The way to be blessed, is to learn to forgive
God provides the way, to help us re-live
Learn to forgive, I appeal to your soul
If you won't forgive, you can't fulfil your role...

The way to receive, is to learn to forgive
There is victory in forgiveness; there is strength when we give
When you overcome unforgiveness, you really start to learn
In your life, you will find, sweet joys are yours to earn!

Nowhere like Home

There is nowhere on earth, like a lovely home...
A place where moral values are taught
A space where love and beauty are sought
A place where God is always first
A space where new born babes are nursed!

There is no where on earth, like a happy home...
A place where we teach each other in love
A space where we trust in God above
A place where we often learn to laugh
A space where we learn to give our all, and not a half!

There is no where on earth, like a blessed home...
A place where, joys will never end
A space where, we always learn to be friend
A place to kneel and a place to heal
A space to feel, God's love is real!

There is no where on earth, like a peaceful home...
A place where our parents, owe no rent
A space where all we have, is heaven sent
A place where songs of praises ring
A space to pray, to Christ our King!

There is no where on earth, like a loving home
A place we learn to do our chores
A space where endless love outpours
A place where kids grow up so fast
A space to conquer the devil at last!
Oh! What a blessed home!

The Power of Poems

There is a poem, for every situation in life!
Words to soothe one's mind, and hinder strife-
Words of comfort and words of love
How fresh they come, from the beak of a dove...

Some sing songs, and some write words!
Some will draw some beautiful birds
Poems are words of healing; words that feels
All human pain and tears and needs...

Poems are words of warmth, and words that calms!
Words of joy and strength like psalms-
Words of courage and words of hope
to remove your sorrows, and help you cope...

Some speak words that hurt and words of curse!
While some speak words from bible verse-
Words can stress and words can mess
Let love and peace, your heart harness...

Poems captivate soul and mind!
Leaving no trails of pain behind
With tender words, scars are removed
With overwhelming joy, hearts are renewed!

Achieving Success

Some shine early, some shine late
Work with God, don't get irate
Deep inside, we have something great
So, go for it, and don't you wait!

You may start late, but dare to dream
Don't get cold feet and fail to beam
Do your test, and be the best
In the north, south, east and west!

Persevere, push away your fear
Victory, is oh, so near
Fight for what you want my dear
Opportunities come, then disappear!

Some are laughed at, some are mocked
Some work hard, 'till others are shocked
Negative people, keep them blocked
'till sweet success, your soul has rocked!

You can't have your cake and eat it too
You can't be lazy and still get through
Study, even if your eyes get black and blue
Stick closer to God, like paper and glue

Many are called, but chosen are few
Wear old clothes, 'till you wear new
Stand up tall like Great Miss Lou
Humble calf, drink good milk too.

My God will see you through, for true!

Factual Reflections

The tears you cry today
And the feelings of dismay
Will help you find joy tomorrow
Because God's eyes are on the sparrow

The defeat that you feel today
And the thoughts in disarray
Only occurs to help you find
That success awaits of greater kind

The disappointment you experience today
After the affairs of yesterday
Comes only just to lift your feet
From hopelessness and stress beneath

The struggles of today
Will bring fulfilment your way
For how boring life would be
without the challenges that we see.

Use Your Talent

Working so hard each day and night
And loving God, with all my might
Using the potentials, he placed in me
To bring the glory, Lord to thee!

A talent buried, is of no effect
A talent never used, will have defect
For when God was handing out each gift
He made the way for man's burden to lift!

For what purpose is a talent, that is never shared
And what is the value, of a life not prepared
To touch someone at his point of need
In order to, help him succeed!

A Talent is a Gift

A talent wisely used
Can never be refused
Use your talent, use it well
You may keep a soul from hell!

A talent is a gift
Use it well and swift
You did not choose it, but don't refuse it
Without it, in this life, you will not fit!

A talent buried in deceit
Leads to a life of painful defeat
To refuse your gift is so unfair
To a God whose love is so sincere!

On the Edge of Greatness

It started one day, with a single dream
And as I ponder, sitting by the stream
My thoughts went wild, thinking, how could it be
In tears of awe, I could not see
That I was standing, on the edge of greatness!!!

Muscling the courage, to see this dream come through
I learn to be determined, devoted, kind and true
I had to pass some barriers, internal and external
In order to achieve, God's gift to me eternal
Now, I am standing, on the edge on greatness!!!

All this time, the gift of God, was tightly wrapped in me
Waiting for release, when I give my all to thee
Thinking I'm so feeble, from challenges I ran
But the patient Lord and Saviour, keep telling me, "I can"
For I am standing, on the edge of greatness!!!

All my hopes and dreams, I gladly give to him
For the gracious Lord of Glory, took me out of sin
Standing on the mountain, I just keep on winning
For God was telling me, from the very beginning
That I was standing, on the edge of greatness!!!

Believe in Yourself

Believe in yourself, to achieve your goal
If you won't, you may fall in a hole
Relying on others, may make you a victim
Trust in God, he'll be your support system!

Don't seek encouragement, from family and friends
Your privilege for success, proudly God defends
Dare to be an eagle, dare to fly alone
Soar to heights of honour, fearing not the zone!

Be careful, in how you share your dream
Negative ones may laugh at you and scream
Words of grave unkindness, that hurts you deep within
Rise above them; with faith in God, you win!

Reach for your bright tomorrow
Although today, you may feel sorrow
No one on earth can stop you now
Believe in yourself, and take a royal bow!

Poems Bursting in My Head

I was sitting by the watershed
When poems, started bursting in my head
I rushed, to write them down
Words of adjectives, verbs and noun__

I smelt, the sweetest scent
The cool wind, told me what it meant
It was the fragrance of grace
That came to be my brace__

I was captured, by the moment
Wrapped, in the love of God's atonement
As time passed quickly by
Singing birds said, "Night was drawing nigh" __

My thoughts were running wild
and I felt like such a child
Then heaven sent the sprinkling rain
To gently touch my dreaming brain__

When Your Rubber Meets Your Road

For relationships to stay alive
In God's word, please take a dive
For in his laws, we find our guide
To a victorious life, in which to hide-

It takes more than good shape, and pretty face
To cement a relationship, and keep it in God's grace
For when you think you cannot cope
God let down his victory rope-

When life's challenges cave you in
The power of God will make you win
You dare not rely on your own strength
We need God's arm, at its full length-

Humble yourselves, and never you boast
God's protection, will be at your door post
For when your rubber meets your road
Only God, can lift your heavy load-

Value Your Relationship

Is your relationship worth anything?
Look at your finger, see the beautiful ring!
Your life is what you make of it
So, you both should take the time to knit...

Do you value your relationship?
Or does it feel like a beating whip!
Put peace, respect and love there-in
Throw hurts and unforgiveness in your bin...

Did you enter your relationship in a blind fold?
Then sadly watch it getting cold!
There is still hope for you my friend
Pray, God will help you to the end...

Does despair attack, and take a grip?
To the altar of God, please take a trip!
He will relieve your dreadful load
And lead you on to victory road...

What Goes Up Must Come Down

Before a tree start bearing fruit
Its significance is not felt
But when it starts to bear good fruit
All around it; people dwell!

Like a tree, out in the wild
You may be ignored, or treated like a child
Despite the clouds that come your way
Do not ever get dismayed

For the God who sits so high above
Will fill you with his tender love
Don't wait for man to acknowledge you
Stay focused on what you were born to do!

The things disregarded today
Will be greater needed in another way
For what goes around, must come around
And what goes up, must come down!

Nothing's Impossible

A tree starts out small
But gradually grow tall
A life in a ditch
Can become so rich...

A bird in the bush
Is not one you can push
The life in your care
Is the one to hold dear...

If you started out poor
You can be sure
All will be well
When you ring God's bell...

The smallest axe, chops down big tree
You can move mountains on your knee
Believe you can
And you will stand...

Nothing's impossible for a black man
Is in the "White House," carving out big plan
If you ever dare, to start dream big
No one can spin you, like a gig...

Through the Eyes of a Poet

The power of words is known
And the kindness always shown
Through language that is clean
is very often seen
through the eyes of a poet-

The child that almost dies
and the parents who agonize
with hearts of love and fears
are seen with eyes of tears
through the eyes of a poet-

When emotions make you swell
and in peace, you cannot dwell
The hands you need to hold
can be seen now through the cold
through the eyes of a poet-

No matter what situations come
to hold you at ransom
The way you can be free
is the one that's always seen
through the eyes of a poet-

The love you need to find
is not in any mankind
Right where you are situated
is sweet hope communicated
through the eyes of a poet-!

Nursing

Nursing is a kind and compassionate job
If I did anything else, my soul I would rob
Right here in the thickness of the night
Caring for my patients, is feeling so right!

Nursing is said to be a "calling"
To help someone, who from health is falling
On the ward, sometimes there is bawling
But in my heart, a fresh peace is installing!

Nursing is not just a job of choice
For each patient's right, we are the voice
While we work, we keep our patients cheered
Thanking God for those lives that have been spared!

Nursing is certainly my heart beat
Keeping me loving, warm and discrete
There's nothing else I'd rather be
Than a caring nurse for all to see!

The Language of Poems

Poems speak the language, we all understand
Teaching us the way today, to lend a helping hand
Adding moral values, as we journey through this land
Keeping us pure and strong, for God's Royal Marching Band!

Poems speak the language, we all understand
Giving us the wisdom, to stay off sinking sand
Giving us directives, just how to think or how to stand
So, step by step we walk with God, we raise no magic wand!

Poems speak the language, we all understand
Showing us life's beauty, daily that it scanned
They tell of many cultures, their music and their brand
Showing how God loves us, and that heaven will be grand!

Reading and Writing Poems

Reading and writing poems, brings a feeling
That truly fosters inward healing
It helps us with our daily reasoning
Adding flavour to our lives, oh yes, it's seasoning!

Reading and writing poems, is so appealing
We are lifted from the ground to the ceiling
Relieving stress, it adds new meaning
We feel such hope, it's like we're dreaming!

Reading and writing poems, keeps me a kneeling
For my doubt and fears, it is always peeling
It keeps me from dishonest dealing
So, I cannot harbour hatred or stealing!

SEX

Sex cannot be naked
It needs protection and love
It needs the softest clothing
Being sent from high above!

Sex cannot be lonely
It needs companionship and joy
It should not be treated careless
For sex is not a toy!

Sex should not be abused
It's for married couples only
It must not be loosely handled
Or you may end up lonely!

Sex is not a hobby
You must have control
Let us not erode it
We must keep it whole!

Sex needs care and comfort
From the person that is yours
Therefore, you should be faithful
In all romantic chores!

Sex must be clothed with dignity
It needs trust, love and respect
If not, it will explode
What else do you expect!

Sex needs security
In an atmosphere of love
This is the way it prospers
With no hatefulness or shove!

This Poem Tree

I feel a tree of poems, growing inside my belly
It feels so fresh and fine, it's like coconut jelly
As this tree so graciously grows
It keeps me standing on my toes.

This poem tree is a gift of life
Blessing each husband and each wife
It is springing up so fresh in me
Spilling warmth and love, I see

It is a strong tree with many branches
And each poem is a branch that glances
Upon the pains and tears of man
To blow healing wind, just like a fan.

Do you need healing? Check this tree.
Do you need blessing? Fall on your knee.
Though in me; this tree is not mine
This tree is from God, it is divine
Believe in each stanza and each line.

The Niagara Falls!

The Niagara Falls flows powerful and so right
Separating two countries, and it looks so white
It is sparkling, and so beaming bright
As we behold it, all through the day and night!

The Niagara Falls beats incessantly and strong
I wish everyone in the world, would just come along
And see its glory, flowing all day long
When I saw it, I was happy, I sang a worship song!

The Niagara Falls is not like any other falls
It sounds like music, when your name it calls
The mist forms like a mountain, this is true, not false
When children visit, they don't drive you up the walls!

Take the boat ride, or view it from Sane Tower
You will experience the bliss of its power
The scenery is nice with rainbow and sun-flower
I will never forget Niagara Falls; it thrills me every hour!

Niagara Falls caused all my fears to cease
When God spoke to me and gave me sweet release
And there in the moment, I found such joy and peace
Thinking of Niagara Falls make joyful thoughts increase!

God must be strategic, to make this Falls so high
No one can climb it; no need to ask me why
It was made for a purpose, this we can't deny
It has blessed so many, as each day goes by!

My Children

My son is my prince; my daughter is my princess
As Christians, they represent His Royal Highness
I pray they'll walk in love, humility and oneness
God will help my children and cover them with brightness!

Thank God for my children, I love them dearly
The qualities they show are displayed so rarely
They rise to bless their parents and do it sincerely
Now that they are far away, we visit them yearly!

We give God all the Glory; we give God all the Praise
For without his mercy, our arms we could not raise
And without his kindness; we have no appraise
So grateful for these children; they keep our love ablaze!

Let's bless each other's children and help them to achieve
And guide them in their thinking and see what's up their sleeve
Help them speak with confidence, so that they believe
Faith in God, with hard work, bring success they receive!

Troubles Come and Troubles Go!

Troubles come and troubles go, because they cannot last
Don't worry about the future, nor stress about the past
Give God all your worries and learn to pray and fast
God will always help you; his power is so vast!

Problems come and problems go, as they're often solved
Sometimes they rise like mountains, but quickly are dissolved
They make life distressful, so why have they evolved
Problems teach us lessons, so around them, all revolved!

Struggles come and struggles go, they are a part of life
They mould in us character; ask an honest wife
The way we handle them, can keep away the strife
That often comes to haunt us, cutting like a knife!

Challenges come and challenges go, so why be so alarmed
In an atmosphere of worship, the devil has been disarmed
Trust in God and focus; no one can get you harmed
With scripture, prayer and worship, we are always armed!

The Sun Will Shine Again!

The sun will shine again, so wipe away your tears
In humble, sweet surrender, give God all your cares
He knows all about it, but tell him, anyway
God is always listening, call on him today!

The sun will shine again, don't focus on your pain
Christ will ease the burden, and cleanse away all stain
If you learn to trust him, when shadows lurk around
With gladness, you'll discover, the victory you have found!

The sun will shine again, though burdens weigh you down
If you stay obedient, you will wear a crown
For God in heaven looks down, on all man's pain and ills
And he quickly reaches out, to help us climb up hills!

The sun will shine again, don't you ever doubt God
He is waiting on you, to reach out and take your rod
Be comforted my people, I know you all, too well
I'll rescue you from Satan, and shield your soul from hell!

The sun will shine again, see the rainbow in the sky
In spite of all the darkness and fogs that passes by
At the end of each experience, great wisdom does unfold
For God in His Supremacy, has Glory, to behold!

You have to let them go!

When the time has come
We have to let them go
Yes, you love your children
But you have to let them go!

When the time has come
You really have to show
You can't always keep your children
You just have to let them go!

When the time has come
And your children sweetly grow
On their own, they have to stand up
You just have to let them go!

When the time has come
And your children get mature
Some may want to stay
But you have to let them go!

When the time has come
And your children are moving slow
You know you've grown them well
Tell them, you have to let them go!

When the Time has Come

When the time has come
Don't try to keep your children down
How will they ever learn
To reach for their own crown!

When the time has come
Let your children shine
For if you ever stop them
You might visit them in shrine!

When the time has come
Don't act as if you're blind
If you don't guide your children
You will leave them far behind!

When the time has come
Help your children to step out
When you trust in God
There is nothing you can doubt!

When the time has come
Give your kind support
When your children call you
They will give you glad report!

As I Reflect

As I reflect and care for others
God led me to pray for my sisters and my brothers
I prayed for the weak, the sick and hospitalized
Also, the wounded, hurting and victimized!

As I reflect, I see God's love for all
Throughout summer, winter, spring and fall
I prayed for gunmen, rapist, murderer and thief
Also, musicians, record holder, politicians and chief!

As I reflect, may all people live as one
In this way, the victory would be won
Let's make effort to love and forgive
Making it possible for each one to breathe and live!

As I reflect, I feel a lot of hope
God's love will guide and daily help us cope
Accepting each other, makes us sweet and warm
We would live so good, no one would dare to harm!

Chapter 8

Friends & Friendship

A Very Outstanding Friend

You have been a kind and caring friend
And I'm so proud of you
I'm thrilled by your commitment
This is found in just a few!

You have been a gracious, fulltime friend
In this special friendship we have grown
You have blessed me with your kindness
I am so pleased to make it known!

You have been a warm and precious friend
Reaching out; with your caring touch
As I reflect on all your goodness
I appreciate you so much!

You have been a very outstanding friend
Each day; your warmth is still the same
I love you and I thank you
"Most Wonderful" is your name!

My Kind and Caring Friend

You have been a kind and caring friend
I'm praising God for you!
I'm blessed by your dedication
This is found in just a few!

You have been a warm and special friend
You treat others like your own!
You have helped me with your kindness
Thanks for not leaving me to walk alone!

You have been a thoughtful and faithful friend
Reaching out to me, with your purest touch!
And as I watch you care for me
My heart keeps thanking you so much!

You have been my most outstanding friend
You stand out among the rest!
In your endeavours and aspirations
I wish you all the very best!

My Warm & Special Pixie!

You have been a real and precious Pixie
I mean every word; it's true
Being fascinated by your dedication
I lift my hat to you!

You have been my warm and special Pixie
Reaching out with your blessed touch
As I see your creative work of Art
I keep thanking you so much!

You have been a true and thoughtful Pixie
Who deserves to be cheered by me
You have thrilled me with surprizes
This gift I give you on my knee!

You have been a co-worker, friend and Pixie
You add sunshine to my days
I think of you with joy and splendour
You are nice in so many ways!

You Have a Friend in Me

On your face, I saw confusion
In your words, I heard despair__
but I am here to tell you
your deliverance is near__

you need to know I love you
no matter what happens__
for everywhere you go
there my love transcends__

There's no need to be downhearted
I'm staying by your side__
Take my hand and squeeze it
We will overcome each tide__

When troubles overtake you
you have a friend in me__
Sometimes, it's through our trials
God's grace and love we see__

My Warm and Loving Friend

God blest the day I met you
My warm and loving friend!
you are so outstanding
On my love you can depend!

All the qualities of a true friend
I found them all in you!
The character of a real man
Gives me the strength to keep so true!

In the freshness of the garden
I want to sit and talk with you!
With voice and heart in oneness
We'll connect like crazy glue!

Baby, if you're ever hurting
I'll be there, in the light or in the dark!
You deserve this special honour
For in my heart, you create a special spark!

My Friend

You always lend a helping hand
As I journey through this land
I never walk on sinking sand
Within this marvellous friendship band!

My friend, my friend, please stay with me
As respect and love is still the key
You are sociable and warm, I clearly see
All the blessings you bring, you charge no fee!

Being with you is my delight
To keep our friendship, we must fight
Sweet thoughts of you I hold so tight
Until my face is twinkling bright!

A Lifetime Friend

I really need a life time friend
One in whom I can depend
A friend to guide me to the end
Despite the trials life may send!

A friend is such a beautiful gift
In troubled times he/she gives a lift
To be a true friend, may I be swift
Between real friends, there is no rift!

By my side you seem so sweet
And in my thoughts, you fit so neat
Oh friend, God's holy word we must repeat
Until in heaven, we sit at his feet!

True Friends

It is certain that, true friends are forever
To achieve their goals; they always endeavour
To help each other, they will go wherever
Good friends go forward, but backwards they never

It is a fact that, true friends stick together
And fight in life, through any stormy weather
If one friend's load feels heavy like a leather
All friends come together, to make it light like a feather

It is proven that, friendship last through the years
In laughter, sadness, pain or tears
Respect and love, is the garment, a true friend wear
This is why he cares and shares!

It is known that friendship is more important than gold
Whether you're fat, slim, young or old
I cannot do without my friends I was told
When I'm with my friends, all our beauty unfolds!

It is a reality that, friends do help with loathsome chores
All their resources, they truly outpour
They pray for each other, before they rush through their doors
Friends are still friends, even if he or she snores!

Just you and me

Hand in hand we walk
Hand in hand we talk
Then sitting by the water brook
We pause a while, and read a book__

Face to face we smile
Face to face, along each mile
Cherishing your tender touch
And oh! I wanted it so much__

Shoulder to shoulder we lean
Shoulder to shoulder we beam
Together we do our work
So, in this way we'll never shirk__

Voice to voice we speak
Voice to voice, throughout each week
For you take away my loneliness
And fill me with such happiness__

Heart to heart we feel
Heart to heart we heal
For closer yet we seek to be
in harmony, just you and me__

I Saw my Friend

I saw my friend in the distance
and wished that she was near
I saw my friend, in the morning
And she was still so dear!

I saw my friend looking lonely
And hoped, she was not cold
I saw my friend in the morning
And she was not so old

I saw my friend, she was praying
I knew she prayed for me
I saw my friend in the morning
Her beauty, I still see

I saw my friend, with eyes of jasper
And oh, she was so fair.
I saw my friend in the morning
And know that she still cares

I saw my friend, looking at me
With love that was so rare
I saw my friend in the morning
And she was still sincere.

Chapter 9

Babies

Welcome, our Bundle of Joy!

Welcome to the world of wonder
Where have you been, we ponder?
We receive you with joy and pride
Our arms of love are opened wide!

Nine months we wait to hold you close
To care for you and wipe your nose
You are such a bundle of joy
Can't wait to buy your first big toy!

So excited to have you here
To kiss your face and keep you near
We thank the Lord for such a gift
We will have fun, as you grow swift!

With tear-filled eyes, we looked at you
Love melted our hearts; you felt it too
Your baby smile is all we need
To keep us strong and warm indeed!

Grateful for Our Baby

Oh, the warmth and joy we felt
As we first saw you, our hearts melt
Praising God with grateful hearts
We loved it when your heartbeat starts!

We'll keep you in the love of God
And just like Moses, stretch your rod
So thankful you are in our life
God's gift to each husband and wife!

Your baby skin is soft and smooth
Each cell and tissue we will soothe
Your mom and dad are here for you
To watch you grow and train you, too!

You warm our hearts and make us smile
We love you so much; all the while
At the end of prayer, we say shalom
Together we make a happy home!

A Precious Pearl

I love my baby's scent
It reminds me, she was heaven sent
This beautiful babe is mine
Her skin is soft and so refine!

I love to relax, and look at her
Joy, in my heart it stirs
God gave me, this lasting gift
I had her, oh, so swift!

Though young and tender, you can see
That you are a special part of me
I love you, with all my heart
We are bonding from the start!

Well, since you're here to stay
Let's keep in God's own way
You light up my whole world
You're such a precious pearl!

You're My Baby

Like a tender gentle vine
You are of a special kind
Touching the deepest part of me
To filter loving over thee
You're my baby...!

Like the cool refreshing breeze
You brought me gently to my knees
The love I feel to have you here
has often filled my eyes with tear
You're my baby...!

Though you cannot talk right now
I know you want to tell me how
in your heart, you love me too
as you smile, when I put on your shoe
You're my baby...!

With my baby, I will cuddle
With every step, we'll always snuggle
All this time, where have you been?
I'm so glad with you I win
You're my baby...!

This Tender Vine

It's worth it all, to have you dear
For you, nine long months, I have prepared
Despite some frightening labour pains
My deepest love for you maintains!

At the first sight of you, my heart melts
With the overwhelming passion, that I felt
With tear filled eyes, I touched your face
As I saw on you, such tender grace!

Deep inside, I felt such peace
It causes my doubts and fears to cease
I know that God is here, with us to stay
even when we grow old and grey!

Can I raise this tender vine?
I must lean on God, who's so divine
No need to wonder if I can
For God has shown to me, his plan!

My Baby Bonder

Welcome my baby "bonder"
Welcome to the world of wonder!
Gazing on you, I ponder
What were you doing over yonder?...

Welcome my baby "bonder"
With you I can't go under!
When you cry, I hear the thunder
No one can put us asunder...

Welcome my baby "bonder"
Caring for you, I make no blunder!
Won't let you fall or plunder
Let me spill on you, some powder...

My Bouncing Baby Boy

Parcelled as a present, is my bouncing baby boy
Given as a gift of life, presented like a toy
Smiling as I looked on him, I quickly named him Roy
This treasure is a lifetime gift, I really can enjoy!

Bundled in a blanket, is my bouncing baby boy
He makes no noise when he is full, he just will not annoy
I whispered in his ear today, your mother's name is Loye
I held him up to burp, after feeding him with soy!

Cradled in my bosom, is my bouncing baby boy
Packaged for a purpose here, God's angels to employ
I will grow him as a soldier, so that Satan can't destroy
Someday, he will leave me, for God's mission to deploy!

__Right now, I love my baby boy__

Loving My Baby

I see sparkle in your twinkling eyes
It feels like paradise
I feel compassion, when you smile at me
Your love is all I see!

I feel "triggers" in your baby touch
I'm loving you so much
I hear the tapping of your heart beat
and the rhythm sounds so sweet!

I feel blessing when you laugh and play
I love my baby comes what may
I will ensure that you're well fed
And that your bed is always spread!

I'll protect your soft and tender skin
Tossing all mosquitos in the bin
You're my darling and my joy
Also, my gracious baby boy!

I'm having a taste of heaven
You can count from one to seven
My baby has the sweetest charms
I'll keep my baby from all harms!

My Baby Boy

As I feed my baby
I see twinkle in his eyes
When I try to bathe him
I hear screaming in his voice!

As I dress my baby
I see love shining on his face
and as I stretch to take him up
He rolled in my embrace!

As I play with my baby
he wiggles up his toes
and when I calm him down to sleep
The cool wind softly blows!

As I see my baby
Love in my heart start flows
And as he changes
I delight to watch him, as he grows!

My Baby Girl

As I see my baby
She is such a special rose
When I try to feed her
She wiggles up her toes...!

As I hug my baby
There's no fear in her eyes
and every time she's wide awake
I lift her to the skies...!

As I bathe my baby
I saw her runny nose
Then I softly wiped it
And quickly put on her clothes...!

As I love my baby
I thank my God for her
She is such a darling
I gently wrapped her in a fur...!

Chapter 10

Birthdays

Happy Birthday My Sister!

Happy birthday my sister, enjoy your special day
You have shown me kindness, in your unique way
You are such a treasure, much more than I can say
May God richly bless you, this I often pray!

Happy birthday my sister, you're such a shining star
Sisters are more important, than house or fancy car
You are understanding, I love the way you are
The values we have shared, are taking us afar!

Happy birthday my sister, the thoughtfulness you show
Kept me motivated, as in God's grace we grow
Regardless of life's struggles, this I surely know
I respect you, more than words can now bestow!

Happy birthday my sister; our friendship has no end
Because of your standard; you will never bend
Anywhere you go; you add a beautiful blend
For you create a bonding, I strongly recommend!

Happy Birthday My Father

Happy birthday my father, this is a wonderful day
You have the heart of kindness that bless me on my way
You have brought me pleasure, by all you do and speak
The memories of your love can never go away!

Happy birthday my father, you are my guiding star
Your presence means more to me than silver, gold or car
You are understanding, I want to sing and play guitar
The guidance you are giving, will now take me afar!

Happy birthday my father, it's the thoughtfulness you show
That keeps me so devoted and loyal, as I grow
In spite of all life's challenges; this you have to know
You have a marvellous daughter that is proud to tell you so!

Happy birthday my father, with pride I call you dad
I'll tell the world, you're the best gift I've ever had
If anyone should hurt you, I'd be really mad
You mean so much to me, and always make me glad!

Happy Birthday my Father

Happy birthday my father, this is your special day
you have shown me kindness, in your own unique way
You are such a treasure, much more than I can say
I know God will always bless you, and for you I pray!

Happy birthday my father, you are my shining star
your love is more important, than house or fancy car
you are understanding, I love it when we par
The values you have taught me, took me from afar!

Happy birthday my father, it's the kindness that you show
that keeps me motivated and strengthened as I grow
regardless of life's struggles, this I surely know
you deserve a deeper respect, than words can now bestow!

Happy birthday my father, I'm so proud to be your son
Everything you prayed about; you can call it done
In radiance and in glory; angels around you shone
Enjoy your special day and do have lots of fun!

Happy Birthday Our Boss!

Happy birthday our boss, the day has gladly come
With joy we have been waiting; to say to you, welcome
To a day of celebration with food, guitar and drum
Because you care for all and surely not just some!

Happy birthday our boss, you're sparkling like a
broach
Your smile is so refreshing, it drives away reproach
You are understanding; with problems we can approach
On this team of staff, you are the greatest coach!

Happy birthday our boss, with cheerfulness you show
That we should work together, when burdens hang down low
Despite all the daily challenges that we undergo
With you we are successful; reaping what we sew!

Happy birthday our boss, you are such a charm
When you are around, no one dare to harm
God has made you special; for you are so warm
Enjoy your special day, from the time your clock alarm!

Happy Birthday My Friend

You have been a smiling and soulful friend
You add meaning to my life
Because of your generosity
I am the happiest wife!

You have been a loyal, full time friend
With you I'm so complete
I feel such excitement
Every time that we meet!

You have been a warm and special friend
We share precious moments through the years
And as we celebrate your birth
My thoughts are filled with cheers!

Happy Birthday my gracious, long-time friend
Our friendship is so nice
I love you and I trust you
We'll keep our friendship filled with spice!

Happy Birthday My Brother

Happy birthday my brother, I bless you on your day
Keep on praising God and trust him all the way
You are a devoted brother; I really have to say
God is truly with you; for you always pray!

Happy birthday my brother, keep shining as a star
Brothers are more precious than money, house or car
You are so supportive; keen and genuine you are
The moral values you uphold, are taking you afar!

Happy birthday my brother, the Godliness that you show
Has kept your face refreshing and whiter than the snow
As you humbly serve the Lord, and daily seek to grow
You are a greater blessing; that keeps me on my toe!

Happy birthday my brother, with pride I call you mine
I'll tell the world around me, you are so refined
We understand each other, and this is just a sign
That God has made the difference, keeping us in line!

Happy Birthday My Dear Wife!

Happy birthday my dear wife
You are such a living rose
And every time I look at you
More love my heart expose!

Happy birthday my darling
You are such a part of me
You make me feel so special
You are the angel I can see!

Happy birthday my friend and lover
This is your special day
I pause to tell you how I love you
In such an extra special way!

Happy birthday my true love
You are the apple of my eyes
The passionate moments that we share
Will take us to the skies!

Because it's Your Birthday

You are sweet, precious and smart
Having such a gracious heart
You're more special, than words can say
Joy fills the air, because it's your birthday-

So proud and grateful for who you are
Being the most radiant, shining star
We love you, in an extra special way
The sun shines, because it's your birthday-

worldwide, there's none quite like you
Always pouring love like glue!
People are tenderly drawn to you
You're so beautiful; because it's your birthday-

You have blest others with kindness
Showing God's love has no blindness
So, stay in happiness, comes what may
Have lots of fun, because it's your birthday-

It's Your Birthday

You are much more special, than words can ever say
A special fragrance fills the air, because it's your birthday
Thanks for the things you've done, whether small or great
I love you even more today, as we celebrate!

My heart goes out for you, in such a loving way
The sun reflects its glory, because it's your birthday
So grateful for who you are, and sacrifices made
You are the living rose; whose beauty cannot fade!

I'm so proud of who you are, material things cannot repay
My heart expands with respect, because it's your birthday
Throughout the world, there's no one quite like you
People are drawn to you; your love is just like glue!

For your long life and strength, to God I always pray
Have lots of fun, because it's your birthday
I'm so blessed, when you're around
You keep my feet firm on the ground!

Happy Birthday My Partner!

Happy Birthday my lover, enjoy this beautiful day
You have changed my life and blest me on my way
I'll take you out with pleasure; love will not delay
You are my sweetest joy; I love it when we play!

Happy Birthday my sweetheart, you're my shining star
Without you as my soul-mate, I could not go far
You are so romantic; I just love the way you are
We are going places, so in love we stay on par!

Happy Birthday my darling, I just have to let you know
That I am fascinated, by all the love you show
We will make pretty babies; so glad to tell you so
You deserve a life of happiness and a wife that always glow!

Happy Birthday my partner, our friendship cannot end
Our love has such affection, I know we will always blend
Anywhere you go, my warmth on you I send
You're always so attractive, I love your stylish trend!

Happy Birthday My Darling!

Happy birthday my darling
I love you oh. so much
I would spend my life around you
Just to feel your caring touch!

Happy birthday my sweetheart
You are such a part of me
The sparkles in your eyes
Shows that we were meant to be!

Happy birthday my lover
This is your special day
Warm romance awaits you
In such an extra special way!

Happy birthday my soul-mate
Today we grow more deeply in our love
And as we plan our future
More love keeps flowing from above!

Happy Birthday my Grandson!

Happy Birthday my handsome grandson
You are my Precious Shining Star
You are so brilliant and outstanding
So excited how you are!

Happy Birthday my loving grandson
Stay humbled, it's God who have you blest
You have made your family proud
You are far above the rest!

Happy Birthday my hardworking grandson
Wow, this is your special day
This humbled gift I give you
For the joys you've brought my way!

Happy Birthday my gracious grandson
Keep doing excellent in your school
Grandma wishes you all the best
As you learn the golden rule!

Happy Birthday

I'll give you the roses, while you are alive
I'll tell you how I love you, since you have arrived
your presence is so gracious, your loving is so warm
you can be so sure, you are my sweetest charm
Have a Happy Birthday!

You are my darling husband, to have and to hold
I cherish you so much, my love will not get cold
We will live our lives in beauty, and if we do get old
We will still maintain our values, as we keep strong and bold
I wish you a happy birthday!

There's no need to get sad and lonely
As my love is devoted to you, only
Hand in hand, with God we walk
with one voice and heart we talk
you deserve a happy birthday!

Happy Birthday Aunt!

You're my aunt, mother confidante and friend
I love you so much, my love has no end
You're a beautiful flower with a special blend
Such grace and beauty, is always your trend!

Aunt, you know me so deeply and well
And all of my challenges, auntie can tell
Sweet memories of aunt just make my heart swell
In your love and your warmness, now sweetly I dwell!

Your passion and values are what I hold dear
Your character and virtue, today is so rare
With God and my aunt, I can live without fear
In every way I know that my aunt always cares!

I celebrate your birth in this special way
I cherish you much more than I can say
Your sacrifices of love; I cannot repay
With all of my love aunt, have a happy birthday!

Happy Birthday my Mother

I' m so proud you are my mother
And I love you oh, so much
Nothing in life can compare
With a mother's caring touch!

I wish for you my mother
A birthday filled with love
I chose this gift with pleasure
For it came from God above!

Have a happy birthday my mother
Each day, my respect for you increases
With pride and joy, you raised me
Thankfulness my heart releases!

I cherish you my mother
And I have to let you know
You are extra special
And my gratefulness I show!

You Are A Special Lady

You are a special lady
You scatter roses everywhere
Filled with social graces
What a difference you make here!

You are a special lady
So royal and divine
Always making great impact
It makes me feel so fine!

You are a special lady
And a treasured gift
You bless the lives of many
With joy my heart valve lift!

You are a special lady
God honours you today
The atmosphere has gentleness
Because it's your birthday!

A Special Lady

You are a Special Lady
You bring sunshine everywhere
For you have such beauty
You are an extra-ordinaire!

You are a Special Lady
Having so much love to share
For everyone who knows you
Know you always care!

You are a Special Lady
You deserve a sparkling crown
You touch the lives of many
Despite life's up and downs!

You are a Special Lady
God loves you all the way
A gentle fragrance fills the air
Because it's your birthday!

Happy Birthday My Dear Wife

Happy birthday my dear wife
you are such a living rose
and every time I look at you
more love my heart expose!

Happy birthday my darling
you are such a part of me
you often make me feel so special
you are the angel I can see!

Happy birthday my friend and lover
this is your special day
I pause to tell you how I love you
In such an extra-special way!

Happy birthday my true love
you are the apple of my eyes
The passionate moments that we share
Will take us to the skies!

Chapter 11

Christmas

Mom, Have a Wonderful Christmas Day!

You are our sweet and dearest mother
We love you like no other
In our lives you are no bother
You're nicer than a sister or brother!

Mom, have a wonderful Christmas day
As we bring great joys your way
We love you comes what may
For your love no price can pay!

Mom, you lift our hearts with pride
As your arms are open wide
In you we can confide
In your love we will abide!

Mom, we're so proud of you
Your kind of love is in a few
God keeps you fresh and new
You are radiant, warm and true!

Christmas Come Now; Just in Time

Christmas come now just in time
Just when mi sad and sour like lime
now mi sweet and talking rhyme
Cause Christmas come now just in time!

Christmas come now just in time
Just when mi broke and neva have a dime
Now mi have money and feeling fine
Fah Christmas come now just in time!

Christmas come now just in time
Just when mi long fi likkle cake and wine
now mi eat until mi refine
Fah Christmas come now just in time!

Christmas come now just in time
when all mi could grow was turpentine
now mi grow some sorrel and pine
Fah Christmas come now just in time!

Christmas come now just in time
Just when mi bawl out, Lord I'm thine
Now mi soul get refreshment from the divine
Cause Christmas come now just in time!

(AYAYAI)

Oh, the Glory of Christmas

Oh, the glory of Christmas
Thrills sweeter and sweeter
The longer I live, the more I feel
The coolness of the nice Christmas breeze!

Oh, the glory of Christmas
Shines brighter and brighter
The longer I look, the more I see
The radiance of the bright Christmas trees!

Oh, the glory of Christmas
Loves deeper and deeper
The more I share, the more I feel
The joy of the sweet Christmas bees!

Oh, the glory of Christmas
Blesses stronger and stronger
The more I do good, the more I receive
Gifts from the kind Christmas seas!

Oh, the glory of Christmas
Tastes nicer and nicer
The more I haste, the more I taste
The sweetness of the nice Christmas teas!

The Beauty of Christmas

The beauty of Christmas, can't be explained
As we worship God, and there exclaimed
That Jesus Christ came on the earth
To show each man, how much he's worth!

The beauty of Christmas, can't be ignored
Human beauty is outpoured
It takes more than decorations
To filter love through generations!

The beauty of Christmas, can't be denied
If you can't see it, you have lied
For nature's majesty speaks so loudly
In splendid beauty, all so proudly!

The beauty of Christmas, can't be removed
You can't mess with things, God has approved
When you take down things man made
Nature's beauty has not swayed!

The beauty of Christmas, can't be hidden
If you try to do this, know it's forbidden
This beauty shines everywhere you go
Just relax, enjoy the flow!

The Joy and Bliss that Christmas Brings

Oh, the joy and bliss that Christmas brings
As we celebrate the birth of the King of Kings
Early in the morning, joy bell rings
How sweetly, each person smiles and sings
There are no broken bones, there's no need for slings!

Oh, the joy and bliss that Christmas brings
To Christ, our Saviour, each one clings
While gold and diamond always bling's
Everybody exchanges kindest things
While we dance and play with musical strings!

Oh, the joy and bliss that Christmas brings
Worship flows like powerful springs
While soaring angels spread their wings
In a path of love, now, each heart swings
If Satan comes, he gets some stings!

I Love the Spirit of Christmas!

I love the spirit of Christmas
It's tender and it's soft
I sit in admiration
And think about it oft!

I love the spirit of Christmas
It's gentle and it's kind
It radiates through people
Making them refined!

I love the spirit of Christmas
It' oneness and it's peace
We forget all about our troubles
Unity does increase!

I love the spirit of Christmas
It's refreshing and it heals
As families come together
No hatred anyone feels!

I love the spirit of Christmas
It's joyful and it's love
Each one puts away his difference
And embrace God's warmth, above!

I love the spirit of Christmas
It's happiness and it thrills
As we celebrate our saviour
We eat and go for more re-fills!

Christmas

Christmas is the most wonderful time of the year
It lifts our spirit and keeps us in high gear
It is such a happy time, no one sheds a tear
For this time of year, is one we hold so dear!

Christmas is the most exciting time of the year
We celebrate God's goodness
and on his grace, we stare
We spread God's love to others
as we clap our hands and cheer
This is the season to remember
as we lose our doubts and fear!

Christmas is the most loving time of the year
It draws us close to Jesus, we know that he is here
Christ's birth was such a pleasure, he was surely born to care
His love and his compassion are filtered in the air!

Christmas is the most precious time of the year
We forgive and love each other, and don't fall in a snare
We can get so busy, but for God we must prepare
Each one is blest by Jesus, for his love is so sincere!

Chapter 12

Mothers

Mother's Love

I love you mom, on this your day!
I love you mom, in a special way
Dear mom, please permit me to say
You are the fairest angel, here today…

I bless you mom, right here, right now!
Growing up, you always show me how
To be myself and daily make my vow
I salute you mother, take a royal bow…

I adore you mom, glad to have you here!
I admire you mom, on your face I stare
Mother never cease to teach us how to share
Mother tear the devil daily, like a bear…

I treat you mom, you're my father's bride!
I cherish you mom, I will stay by your side
I hug you mom, in your love I abide
I'm lost for words; mother's love is so wide…
I love you mother, on Mother's Day
I bless you mother, on Mother's Day
I adore you mother, on Mother's Day
I treat you mother, on Mother's Day
I cherish you mother, on Mother's Day
I hug you mother, on Mother's Day

Mom, I Love it

Mom, I love it when you hold my hand
You explain things so that I can understand
I am glad to be your tender vine
To have you near and call you mine!

Mom, I love it when you comb my hair
With each stroke of love, I feel your care
I feel so special to call you mom
Your love impacts more than a bomb!

Mom, I love it when you prepare my meal
With lots of joy you make me feel
The wealth of love you have inside
That draws me sweetly to your side!

Mom, I love it when you discipline me
For you do it in kindness, I can see
Whatever you do it's for my good
To make me qualitative like I should!

Mom, you're my Icon

You're my mother, father, confidante and friend
I love you so much, it's like "world without end"
When I was aching, my heart you have mend
Such grace and such beauty, your heart always send!

Mom understands me and treats me so warm
When she embraces; I feel all her charm
Sweet memories of mother, like angels now swarm
Thinking of her; I just miss my mom's arm!

All that you taught me; I hold them so dear
Your humility and kindness, today is so rare
The values you taught, help me live without fear
What blessed assurance; my mom was sincere!

Throughout my life, you prayed for my soul
You taught me how, to reach out for my goal
You're my icon, you fulfilled all your role
Your kindness is known, in the north and south pole!

You are Such an Amazing Mother!

You are such an amazing mother
You light up our whole world
Reflecting on your dedication
We conclude, you are a special pearl!

You are such an amazing mother
You have our deepest respect
You gave your all to raise us
Your love has no defect!

You are such an amazing mother
Your values keep us at our best
And it only goes to show
You are "a cut above the rest!"

You are such an amazing mother
You serve with your whole heart
Your qualities are exceptional
We love you from the start!

Happy Mother's Day!

I'm so proud you are my mother
I love you like no other
You have been my dearest friend
One in whom I trust and totally depend!

I'm so privileged you are my mother
Growing up, we bonded closely with one another
In your training and discipline, I found fulfilment
I never stop loving you, not for one moment!

I'm so blessed you are my mother
When you're around you are no bother
You have instilled so many values in me
To ensure I become the best I can be!

I'm so thrilled you are my mother
You have been sister, councillor and brother
Your integrity, character and qualities, I treasure
I love, respect and cherish you beyond measure!

A Special Rose and Icon!

You have been a Special Rose and Icon
You mean the world to me
I'm so thrilled you are my mother
I worship God down on my knee!

You have been a Special Rose and Icon
You are so dear to me
You have raised me with such dignity
Now I am all that I can be!

You have been a Special Rose and Icon
I'm so proud you are my mom
As I reflect on all your kindness
Your love hits me like a bomb!

You have been a Special Rose and Icon
I'm here to honour you today
My respect for you is endless
I love you more than I can say!

What a Special Mother!

You are exceptional, loving and sweet
Mom, you are my warmest heart beat
Enjoy this Mother's Day treat
No one can take your seat!

In times of laughter, pain or tears
You are with me through the years!
You never cease to calm my fears
And show me how to climb all stairs!

What a special mother, feeling so blest
Your love and affection keep me at rest
Mother scores a hundred at each test
My heart feels warm here in my chest!

Mother, I could not ask more of you
You sacrifice so much to see me through
I bless and thank you always, too
God's love in mom I view!

I love you Mother

Words are so inadequate, to express how I love you
In my life, your love keeps fresh and true
you are God's treasured gift to me
I appreciate you, more than you could see!

Thank you so much, my blessed mother
you have been there, for me like no other
it has been your joy to care and share
To help us overcome life's wear and tear!

When things got tough, and I felt down and blue
One thing I could be sure of; I can count on you
I was always covered by your warmth and loving smile
and I often stop to gaze on you, a while!

I cherish you my mother, for the values you impart
you were here with me, right from the very start
because of you, I am successful and feeling so complete
and I want to tell you, mom, that you are so sweet!

No one like my Mother

There's just no one like my mother
I love her like I love no other
Her world is filled with warm delight
In her embrace, I feel so bright!

There's just no one like my mother
She's much closer to me than a sister or brother
Her training made me proud and strong
Following her, I can't go wrong!

There's just no one like my mother
In love and respect, we bond with one another
Godliness and good character she always emphasizes
To make us successful, more holy and wise!

There's just no one like my mother
I could never see her one moment as a bother
Mom, you gave; you love; you sacrificed your all
Today, you are honoured, keep standing so tall!

God Bless You My Mother

My mother is the greatest person on this earth
She cares and guides, ever since my birth!
She leads by example, I admire her so much
Somehow my mother, has the warmest of touch!

Holy, gracious, loving and dedicated, characterize her
The fragrance of her love is sweeter than incense of myrrh!
I trust you and love you, thank God you are mine
Your discipline and wisdom, keep me in line!

You're my hero, my darling and fairest star
Everywhere I go, your love sticks stronger than tar!
My dear mother, I could not ask you for more
You invested your time, labour and strength, I am sure!

The holy bible speaks of mom's virtue and style
Her presence brings peace, in her spirit is no guile!
God bless you my mother, you're the champion I see
With your gracious help, I'll be all I can be!

When I think of Mother

When I think of mother, my heart swells with so much love
I know she's God's gift to me, parcelled from above
My mother is even stronger, than a powerful flying dove
With mom, I feel such calmness, I never have to shove!

When I think of mother, the moonlight splash on me
There in meditation, my thoughts of mom are free
My mother is a champion; she conquers on her knee
Giving God the Glory forever more to be!

When I think of mother, I feel so proud of her
She spoke in faith of things, just as though they were
When Satan comes around, my mom causes a stir
Rebuking every darkness; her speech is never slur!

When I think of mother, I am happy all day long
My mother is a darling, so resilient and so strong
She solves every problem; whenever things go wrong
And instead of quarrelling, my mother sings a lovely song!

Thinking of Mother

I often think of mother
I love her like no other
When she's around, she is no bother
At home, she taught us to love one another!

My mother is my dear friend
To all my needs, she does attend
On her faithfulness, I can depend
Because my mother's loving has no end!

Viewing mother in my mind
I see her looking warm and kind
Without her wisdom, I would be blind
In life, she walks before, I walk behind!

Thinking of mother is feeling sweet
Ever so often, I give her a treat
My mother is awesome and very nice
She keeps our family filled with spice!

On Mother's Day

It's morning time, wake up, it's Mother's Day
I feel so happy, let me shout and say
Mother, for your love, I can't repay
but I'm loving my mother, on Mother's Day!

Rise up, stand up, it's Mother's Day
I have to show her in a special way
Her love is here, in my heart to stay
I'm appreciating mother, on Mother's Day!

Hug her, love her, it's Mother's Day
She's shining bright, just like the sun ray
When mom is around, everything is okay
I'm thanking God, for mom on Mother's Day!

Dress her up, take her out, it's Mother's Day
She's the sweetest rose, with us today
All year long, for us, mother will pray
Yes, I'm loving my mother on Mother's Day!

I honour my mother, on Mother's Day!
I adore my mother, on Mother's Day!
I salute my mother, on Mother's Day!

So Much Love in Mother's Day

There is so much comfort in Mother's Day
I could just sit and look at mom's love all day
In the face of storm, she has such peace
Which quickly cause the winds and rains to cease-

There is so much joy in Mother's Day
And in her arms, we all still want to stay
Mom is such a big bunch of fun
She is far sweeter than an Easter bun-

There is so much victory in Mother's Day
Mom cares for us in such a tender way
Now it's our time to show mom we care
For the kind of love mom has is oh, so dear-

There is so much love in Mother's Day
We bring our gifts and run to say
Mother, you're the sweetest darling, we ever know
Your grace and love your children show-

There is so much beauty in Mother's Day
Stretching from Kingston to Montego Bay
She's a tree of love, we are the fruits
Protecting us, with God's word, she quickly shoots-

There is so much blessing in Mother's Day
No wonder, we celebrate mom, in the month of May
Mother, no one can wear your shoe
For every day your love is so brand new

There is so much hope in Mother's Day
I'll work for her as hard as I may
More kids will start to regard their mom
She leads the way to God's great kingdom-

Happy Mother's Day

MOM

Mom, I'm so blessed, just being your son
Who can compare to you, there is simply none?
You maintain standards, yet you are fun
God bless you for all that you have done!

Mom, I'm so proud; you raised me well
So glad to obey and not rebel
By your side, I love to dwell
Mom, you are the reason I excel!

You taught me how to have self-control
So, in life, I can fulfil my role
Mom, I love you with my heart and soul
Mom and Jesus made me whole!

My mother is the cutest woman in town
She wears a bright and dazzling crown
I've never seen her face with a frown
Mom loves her royal, righteous gown!

My Mother

My mother is ever so warm
Her smile and words are filled with charm
With God and mom no one can harm
I feel love and kindness in her arm!

My mother is ever so nice
Her hands and heart are filled with spice
When she speaks, mom is precise
Her gracefulness will always entice!

My mother is ever so calm
Every day she reads her Psalm
The blood of Jesus is her balm
I see caring wonders in her palm!

My mother is ever so kind
Doing God's Will is on her mind
She never passes anyone like she is blind
For this cause, she was designed!

So proud you are My Mother!

I'm so proud you are my mother
I love you like no other
You have been my dearest friend
One in whom I trust and totally depend!

I'm so privileged you are my mother
At home, we bond closely with one another
In your training and discipline, I found fulfilment
I never stop loving you; not for one moment!

I'm so blessed you are my mother
When you're around, you are no bother
You have instilled so many values in me
To ensure I become the best I can be!

I'm so thrilled you are my mother
You have been sister, counsellor and brother
Your integrity, character and qualities I treasure
I love, respect and cherish you beyond measure!

Mom, you are our hero!

Mom, you are our hero, the champion of our lives
Caring for your children, like queen bee in their hives
You have sons and daughters that are proud to tell you so
Climbing over mountains; mom, with God, you are a pro!

Mom, you are our hero; showing God is above all gods
Fighting like a lion and beating all the odds
You provide for all your children;
being both our mom and dad
You are the greatest blessing, that we've ever had!

Mom, you are our hero; fearing not what others say
You trust in God forever, and in sacredness, you pray
Confronting all Goliaths; mom is victory prone
You are the bravest soldier that we've ever known!

Mom, you are our hero; standing up to every test
Not backing down from Satan, you are the very best
In wisdom and in Godliness, you taught us how to choose
Not one of your children, you would ever lose!

Chapter 13
Fathers

I Love You Dad

Although you were not always around
Your guidance and loving still abound
When we met, the love you have shown
Helped me find strength, now that I'm grown

Thank you, dad, for the good times we shared
I would laugh so loud and touch your beard
Glad to know I'm not disowned
I have a father who is world-renowned

With a genuine father and daughter
There is love like flowing water
As long as you are alive
In confidence, I will arrive!

Just to know, you are my friend
And my rights you will defend
Gives me such warm assurance
And even strong endurance!

-Love You Dad-

Loving My Father

I have come a long way today
Just to wish you a happy Father's Day
Dad, you mean so much to me
I'll shine for you and be the best I can be!

You're a tower of strength, you're excellent
Proving that having me was no accident
There's a child in me still needing dad
And the woman in me is feeling glad!

I don't look like you, but have your height
So, I fight through life with all my might
With your support I stand up tall
For with God and dad, I have it all!

Can I be too old to call you dad?
When you are the best gift, I've ever had
I still love it when you hold my hand
And life's values you let me understand!

You are a Special Gift of God

Dad, you are my greatest earthly hero
Without you, I would be zero
Like a strong and mighty lion
You lead us here in Zion
You are a precious gift of God!

A father is the most precious gift
Not allowing his children to drift
He holds his family together
Regardless of the type of stormy weather!
You are a precious gift of God!

You are defender, shelter and shield
At daddy's feet, we quickly yield
You are leader and centre post
I have to be careful not to boast
You are a precious gift of God!

An outstanding father you will always be
You are the eyes through which I see
Of all fathers, I believe you are the most
Wonderful and caring, so to you, I make a toast
You are a precious gift of God!

Dad, You Are

You are my leader, father and friend
Oh, I will love you dad, to the end
What would I do if you were not here?
My strength is in your love and your care

You are champion, fighter and backbone
Your children will never leave you all alone
For us, you have provided through the years
As I reflect, my eyes are filled with tears!

You are quarter-back, defender and source
With strong arms, you push back evil force
Your protection is our jacket of life support
Now, we're on our way to heaven's court!

You are overcomer, founder and shield
Dad is the fastest man in life's outfield
We love you dad, can't put it all in words
You soar higher than all eagles and birds!

-Love You Dad-

My Kind and Caring Father!

You have been my kind and caring father
And I'm so proud of you
I'm thrilled by your dedication
This is found in just a few!

You have been a gracious fulltime father
Always thinking of your children
You have blessed us with your kindness
You are example to all men!

You have been a firm; yet gentle father
Reaching out; with your caring touch
And as I see your deep commitment
I appreciate you so much!

You have been my warm and loving father
Every day your warmth is still the same
I respect you and I thank you
Your love has brought you fame!

A Kind & Caring Father

You have been a kind and caring father
We're delighted you're our dad!
We're amazed by your dedication
Every day you make us glad!

You have been a nice and humble father
Always thinking of your own!
Your fragrance is your splendour
Thanks for not leaving us alone!

You have been a firm, yet gracious father
Reaching out to us, with your blessed touch!
and as we watch you care for us
Daddy, we keep loving you so much!

You have been a faithful and loving father
We're so blessed being by your side!
As your children, we confirm this
In your love we will abide!

I Was the First

I was the first to prove you fertile
The first to call you dad__
the first to prove your manhood
the first to make you extra glad! __

I was the first to be your offspring
the first seed from your loin__
the first to bear your surname
the first to be treated as a coin

I was the first born of your flesh
the first made of your bone__
the first to make you responsible
the first you could call your own__

I was the first to carry your blood-line
The first with your DNA__
The first to bear your jeans
The first all the family say__

I was your first chance to raise a child
the first to depend on you__
the first to look to you for love
the first to be abandoned, too! __
-Dad, I forgive you-

Thank you, My Father

I stand right here to tell, how I watched you through the years
And as I see your dedication, my eyes are flushed with tears
Thank you so much, my father, I'm so proud of you
You gave your all to raise me, your love is real and true!

Your arms are always wide open, to embrace me in your love
Your heart swell with compassion, as you pray to God above
All the qualities of a father, I find them all in you
Your kind of thoughtfulness and care, come from just a few!

Dad, I proudly came to tell you, I love you oh, so much
In your love, I found my strength; for your love is of such
Dad, while growing up, I could not ask you to do more
You led me by God's standard, you were faithful, I am sure!

Thanks for being my father, councillor and friend
The principles you outlined, will guide me to the end
I salute you now my father, take this royal bow
You will always be my father; I bless you here and now!

When I Think of My Father

When I think of my father
The sun shines bright for me
Because I obeyed him
I am all that I can be!

When I think of my father
My love grows tall for him
Beholding his sacrifice
My heart is thankful to its brim!

When I think of my father
I have the widest smile
He has such grace and wisdom
Can't help but love him all the while!

When I think of my father
I honour him in my mind
I take pleasure in blessing him
My father is a special kind!

When I think of my father
My heart is filled with joy
He's exemplary to every girl and boy
He is my father; he does not annoy!

When I think of my father
My thoughts are clean and pure
With God, he will not fail me
He is my dad for sure!

My Father

My father is rich with great resource
To protect his family from evil force
He roars at the devil with a voice so course
By the next morning he gets hoarse!

My father gives lots of jokes
In our side he often pokes
His bicycle has colourful spokes
I often take shelter under his cloaks!

My father is always firm and frank
Being filled with Godliness in his tank
Thanking God when he ate and drank
Piles up Praise and Worship in his bank!

My father is a great big bunch of fun
He plays tricks and loves to run
At home, he shines like the glorious sun
Thank you, dad, for all you've done!

My Father is

My father is ever so warm
His touch and words inflict no harm
The gospel of Christ is dad's firearm
And Satan's darts, he will disarm!

My father is ever so great
He guides us how to choose a soul-mate
Also, to trust in God and always wait
Until grace and mercy flies the gate!

My father is ever so keen
We can't do wrong without being seen
We thought his discipline was so mean
Now, on his shoulders, we just lean!

My father is ever so kind
His children are always on his mind
He instilled values each time we dined
To ensure we grow up so refined!

My Dad Got Married

My dad got married for companionship
And thought on life, he'd make a good grip
But, all his money, his wife would rip
I'm taking him for a very long trip!

My dad got married with a beautiful ring
At the reception, we all had to sing
It felt like such a wonderful thing
As we thought, great joy his wife would bring!

My dad got married with thoughtful plans
Of how he'd bless us with his hands
He had so many treasures, even lands
But his wife leaked it all, like grains of sands!

My dad got married with so much hope
He wanted a wife to help him cope
They would bathe each other and lather with soap
Now, dad is sliding down a slope!

The Day You Marry My Father

The day you marry my father
My happiness felt complete
I couldn't bear to see him lonely
Or living life in defeat!

The day you marry my father
Everything inside me came alive
Peace and joy flowed over
I saw my dad revive!

The day you marry my father
I felt excited and so free
Since mom died, he's always grieving
You brought healing; I agree!

The day you marry my father
New meaning filled my life
I can breathe and smell the roses
My dad has a brand-new wife!

Printed in Great Britain
by Amazon

16080829R00181